HOW TO PRA
SPIRITUAL GROWTH

To Maw and Shirley,

God love you,

Ched Dobs

THEODORE E. DOBSON

How to Pray for Spiritual Growth

A PRATICAL HANDBOOK OF INNER HEALING

PAULIST PRESS
New York/Ramsey

Library of Congress
Catalog Card Number: 81-83182

ISBN: 0-8091-2419-x

Published by Paulist Press
545 Island Road, Ramsey, N.J. 07446

Printed and bound in the
United States of America

Contents

Contents

Part Three
Healing of Memories

Appendices

This book is affectionately dedicated to
Barbara Shlemon
who first brought me into the mystery
of the healing love
of Jesus and His Mother,
and who has become
a beloved friend

Acknowledgements

It is with deep gratitude in my heart that I mention the names of the people who have assisted me in writing this book. First and foremost, my thanks goes to my devoted typist and dear friend, Madeline Streich, for preparing the manuscript with a devotion and precision that could only come from love. My deepest thanks goes to Dennis and Matthew Linn, S.J., whose thoughtful encouragement for my writing and other work has always been present when I needed it the most. I am deeply grateful to Patricia Battle, not only for her helpful comments on the manuscript, but also for her loyal friendship. My special thanks goes to Serge Guislain, whose detailed and expert commentary on the manuscript assisted me to clarify my thought in innumerable sections of the book, and to his wife, Jessamine, whose friendly encouragement brought joy into the more difficult moments I encountered while writing the manuscript. And I am most grateful to those friends all over the country, too numerous to mention by name, whose prayers, love, and practical assistance brought me through the difficult experiences of 1980.

Ted Dobson

Foreword

Ten years ago the healing of traumatic memories was largely left to professional therapists using psychological skills but little prayer, or to good-willed Christians using prayer but little psychological skill. Much healing occurred in both cases, but not as much as occurs now when the power of prayer is combined with psychological wisdom. Today professionals such as the twelve hundred belonging to the Association of Christian Therapists combine their professional skills with inner healing prayer similar to that described in these pages. They find that their time seems to be cut by a quarter or more when therapy is integrated with prayer. When Dr. Manuel Soria combined prayer with therapy in one mental institution, thirty-nine out of forty chronic psychotic patients were released. He and others find that as a person develops a real relationship with Jesus Christ through healing prayer, many of the problems of transference and termination are solved, since Jesus and not the therapist becomes the center of a person's life.

But the major growth of healing prayer in the last ten years has been among people who are already emotionally stable and desire to live a more loving life. The churches are rediscovering the power of healing prayer when used in conjunction with in-depth confession, scriptural study, marriage encounter dialogues, directed retreats, and journals. Prayer used in the context of such exercises heals the subconscious so that a person can be more free to give and receive love. Everywhere there is a hunger to learn how to pray, especially with the Scriptures and events in one's life. Retreat houses empty ten years ago now have waiting lists for retreats.

Anyone, then, who has a hunger for more peace or for deeper prayer will profit from Rev. Ted Dobson's ten healing prayers. He draws on the Scriptures, psychological wisdom, and years of experience both in receiving and in offering healing prayer. He avoids the traps of being cloyingly religious or pedantically psychological, of focusing on feeling better rather than on experiencing a deeper lived commitment to Jesus Christ and to others, and especially of introspection rather than looking constantly to Jesus and His reaction.

This is not just a theoretical book nor is it only a witness to one person's unique religious experience. Rather, each chapter unfolds a specific prayer form with its theoretical and scriptural background, an actual case of its use, and a sample prayer to act as a guide to the beginner. The study questions, bibliographies, and appendices are full of suggestions for personal reflection, praying these prayers with a group, or praying these prayers in ministry to individuals.

The temptation will be to read this book straight through for its information rather than slowly praying through the pages. An ideal method would be to read only one chapter at a sitting and to take at least ten minutes to pray the chapter's closing prayer slowly. This is a book not only for one's notes on how to pray but also for one's life by actually praying. Perhaps Paul's prayer for us is an ideal way to begin:

> Out of His infinite glory, may God our Father give you the power through the Spirit for your hidden self to grow strong, so that Christ may live in your hearts through faith, and then, planted in love and built on love, you will with all the saints have strength to grasp the breadth and the length, the height and the depth; until, knowing the love of Christ, which is beyond all knowledge, you are filled with the utter fullness of God. Glory be to Him whose power, working in us, can do infinitely more than we can ask or imagine;

glory be to Him from generation to generation in the Church and in Christ Jesus for ever and ever. Amen (Eph. 3:16–21).

Matthew Linn, S.J., and
Dennis Linn, S.J.
December 12, 1980

Preface
Spiritual Growth and Inner Healing

What the Scriptures Say

"On that day you will understand that I am in my Father, you in me and I in you" (Jn 14:20). With these words Jesus explains to us His world view, the way He sees the world put together. And with these words He also gives to us the motivation and the goal for which to pray for spiritual growth.

To grow spiritually means to experience our being in Jesus and His being in us, and, because of our close relationship with Him, to begin an intimate relationship with the Creator, the source of all Goodness, Beauty, and Truth, because we live in Jesus who has this relationship first. By maintaining our relationship with Jesus in every way we can—that is, by giving our lives to Him, by dedicating all we have and are to Him, by sharing with Him all the faculties of our inner selves and physical selves, by opening to Him our pasts and allowing Him to guide our futures—we come not only to understand who we are as children of God but also to *live* in the power and the glory of that relationship which is our primary identity.

Although all Christians are children of God through Baptism and faith, not all Christians seem to *know* who they are, nor do they seem to live in that precious identity. Rather, the lives of many seem to show little fruit of the dramatic change that happened to them when they were reborn in Christ. These people live in powerlessness when confronting evil and suffering; they seem to be controlled by various destructive patterns of behavior; they do not derive the great amount of life that God offers us through the Scripture, Sacraments, personal prayer, and Christian community. This way of living is not God's dream for us.

Paul teaches us that "when we were baptized into Christ Jesus we were baptized into his death . . . so that as Christ was raised from the dead . . . *we too might have a new life*" (Rom 6:3, 4b, emphasis mine). Inner healing prayer is one way to see fulfilled in our lives the spiritual growth that this Scripture promises, that is, it is a way to *experience* new life in us. As Paul says a little further on, "*We must realize* that our former selves *have been* crucified with him to destroy this sinful body and to free us from the slavery to sin" (Rom 6:6, emphasis mine). But how are we to realize this truth? How are we to obey Paul's injunctions in his other Epistles, for example, ". . . you must kill everything in you that belongs only to earthly life: fornication, impurity, guilty passion, evil desires and especially greed. . . . You have stripped off your old behavior and your old self, and you have put on a new self . . ." (Col 3:5a, 9–10a)?

Inner healing prayer is a way to experience the power and love of Jesus so strongly, personally, intimately, and specifically in various areas of our inner lives that we (often dramatically) experience spiritual growth: What is not of Jesus dies and He lives in us ever more perfectly. Prayers that help us discover our true selves, free our true selves, and heal our memories (this is not the only way to categorize inner healing prayers, but it is a way I find most helpful) reveal to us the truth of our Baptism: that Jesus has always been with us, has never abandoned us, and is constantly working within us to bring us to the perfection He so clearly sees is our destiny. Of course, that perfection will be fully attained only in heaven, the final stage of our spiritual growth, but it is obvious from the words of Jesus and Paul quoted above that we are meant to begin to experience it right now.

Inner healing prayer, then, is one way God uses to make Baptism a living experience of power to change the very fabric of our lives. On our own we cannot put on new selves or strip off our old selves or kill everything in us that belongs only to earthly life; those things are possible only by the grace of God. Inner healing prayer is a means by which God gives us His grace in specific areas of our lives and in specific moments recorded in our memories to help us grow spiritually and obey these injunctions of the Christian life.

Through inner healing, therefore, we can reach the natural goal of the Christian life: "so that . . . we too might have a new life" (Rom 6:4b), or, as Jesus phrased it, "On that day you will understand that I am in my Father, you in me and I in you" (Jn 14:20). As we are healed within, the Spirit of God, planted in us when we were baptized, surges through every part of our lives to unleash His comfort, power, and Love, although this growth does not happen entirely all at once, but little by little. Thus we come to know that Another lives within us, and in Him and using His gifts we can build the Kingdom of God on earth.

Definitions of Inner Healing

Thus we can see that inner healing is a way of experiencing salvation on a day-to-day basis, for it is a way of allowing the new nature or the new self to "progress toward true knowledge the more it is renewed in the image of its Creator" (Col 3:10b). By freeing our inner selves to be renewed in the image of our Father, our hidden selves can grow strong and can be filled with the utter fullness of God (cf. Eph 3:16–19). Salvation is a God-given gift, and when it comes it is given totally and completely; but the paradox is that the work of salvation in us grows as we grow in Christ. Since inner healing is a way of allowing Christ ever more freedom in every part of our lives, it is a way we can ever more completely experience the power of our salvation.

Agnes Sanford has said that healing is a continuing of the creative power of God, a flow of divine energy that repairs that which has been broken and frees that which has been bound. Inner healing, then, is Jesus coming to a hurting person, often through the power of prayer, and sometimes through the mediation of another person, to confront the destructive effects of evil in that person's life, and to recreate that person more completely in the image of God. Jesus heals through the grace of His love, His comfort, His forgiveness, and His challenges so that we can grow more completely into the image that God has of us.

Inner healing is also, to a great extent, learning how to be honest with God, sometimes for the first time in our lives. When we hide our true selves from Jesus we present to Him a mask, a creature He does not know because it is not His creation but rather our own. Since He does not know it, He can neither love it nor heal it; and it is we who have tied His hands because we have not been honest with Him. When, however, we strip that mask from ourselves and simply and honestly tell Jesus the truth about our lives, we are inviting Him into us; and when He comes to us He *must* help us, not because we request or deserve His help, but because it is His nature to help, although the help He gives is that which He sees we need, not necessarily that which we want. Prayers for inner healing help us to become honest and thus allow the Healer to do what is natural for Him.

Inner healing is nothing new to Christianity. The name may be new, and the terms by which we explain it are contemporary, but the kernel of the experience is as old as the healing stories of Jesus and the writings of Paul, whom we have quoted above in relationship to praying for spiritual growth through inner healing. Jesus ministered inner healing with the woman at the well (Jn 4:1–38), with the sinful woman who anointed Him (Lk 7:36–50), with the boy who was possessed by an evil spirit (Mk 9:14–32), with the paralyzed man who was brought to Him (Mt 9:1–8), and with many others.

Inner healing, therefore, is part of the heritage of our forefathers in the Church. The *Confessions* of St. Augustine is a type of personal journal in which he recorded many experiences of what we would call inner healing through healing of memories. *The Spiritual Exercises* of St. Ignatius of Loyola was the first great spiritual work to describe some forms of prayer that we use today in inner healing ministry. The masterpieces of St. John of the Cross and St. Theresa of Avila, which these writers say clearly were written for common folk and not just for cloistered monks and nuns, describe a path we can identify as one of inner healing and finding the true self.

The human potential movement and the science of humanistic psychology, while not the same as inner healing, maintain a definite relationship to it. While these titles comprise a broad and complex field with many different schools and points of view, we can say generally that one of the goals of those groups is knowledge of the human person, and another is awareness of the inner workings of the person; and one of the goals of therapy is freedom for the inner person to be whole. The great difference between them and inner healing is, however, that while they proceed by human wisdom and human relationship alone, inner healing uses these aided and amplified by divine gift.

The strength of these fields and forms of therapy is that they make us aware of the inner realities of human beings; however, they run the risk of teaching us to focus on ourselves for our own sake, and in so doing they can lock us into the limitations as well as release the potentials of human nature. Inner healing, on the other hand, can lead us to see that God, not we, is the center of the universe, and that when we come into proper relationship with Him our twisted lives become whole, for He is unlimited in Himself and in His Love for us. The weakness of inner healing is that it can seem, when it is not properly understood, to provide to our problems solutions that are "too spiritual"; thus, it can encourage people who do not understand it to avoid looking realistically at experiences like feelings, which many people would rather avoid.

Our feelings, however, are not the center of the world either, and when we mistakenly view our world as centered on ourselves we have nothing secure on which to base our lives, and so we fall apart. But when the Holy One is at the center of our feelings and experiences, because He truly *is* the center of Life, our broken lives can come together.

Inner healing, because it is a form of prayer in which Jesus gently guides people to see themselves in the Light of His Love, can lead us into spiritual growth and wholeness. The witness of many professionals in the psychological field who have come to practice therapy in the light of inner healing says that, while psychology does much good, on its own it can lead people into as much bondage as that from which it tries to free them. But when psychology is practiced with Jesus at its center, when the expertise of the competent professional is the means through which Jesus is allowed to work, real and lasting freedom from bondage is possible. Inner healing prayer and sound psychology together truly become God's therapy for broken human lives.

Definition of Terms

To continue learning about inner healing we must address the topic with a common understanding of who human beings are and how we are put together, as well as a common understanding of the terms we use to describe human beings. The picture presented here is not the only way to view the nature of the human person, and other people may choose another way because of their backgrounds or needs. But I choose this understanding because it is psychologically sound as well as scriptural, and because it explains things we need to know both for our healings and for spiritual growth.

However, we need to keep in mind that any presentation of who human beings are is a logical construct and not the reality in itself—that is, these words we will use are mental categories that will help us to understand the reality of our inner selves; but in reality we are not made "in parts" but rather as a unity. Yet these words do refer to realities within us. Each category, however, is not an airtight compartment, for words are limited in their ability to express the truth.

First, the *human person* comprises body, mind (or psyche, from the Greek word *psyche*, which literally translated means "mind" or "soul"), and spirit. Thus, in this book, the words *psychological* and *psychology* refer to things of the mind, especially as distinct from things of the spirit (cf. Heb 4:12); and the term *inner self* refers to the mind and the spirit together.

The *mind* or psyche has several functions: *intellect* (with which the mind perceives truth, reasons, categorizes), *will* (with which it evaluates, decides, and puts decisions into action), *imagination* (with which it puts things together in new ways, creates, and from which come the emotions), and *memory* (with which it records and stores all personal past events, waking or sleeping, just as they happened, with all the thoughts, feelings, and decisions associated with those events, whether or not we may want them recorded and stored).

The *spirit* has several functions also, which correspond to three of the functions of the mind: *communion* or worship (the desire and ability to contact God and adore Him with love and praise), *conscience* (the ability to decide right from wrong and to do what we decide), and *intuition* (the ability to perceive spiritual realities and to understand the truth of the spiritual world).

Both the mind and the spirit can and do exist in states of *consciousness* and *unconsciousness;* in other words, we are aware of only part of what is happening in either of them at any given time.

The *new self* (a term to which we have already referred through the writings of Paul) is a reality of our spirits and it comes to us in Baptism; it is the human spirit that is a child of God, that is in touch with God, and that believes and lives the Truth. Conversely, the *old self* is the human spirit that lives as a child of the world or of Satan, that is out of touch with God, and that believes and lives falsehood and lies about self, the world, and God.

The *true self* (a term to be used frequently in this book) is both a spiritual and a psychological reality; it is everything that the new self is plus the psychological consequences of it—that is, a person's true thoughts, feelings, and the desires of his or her heart. And again, conversely, the *false self* is everything that the old self is plus the psychological consequences of it—that is, all our wrong attitudes and ideas about life, the inability to know our own feelings, and all evil desires.

The ideas of body, mind, and spirit expressed above can be found, described in great detail with scriptural references for each, in Watchman Nee's *The Spiritual Man* (Christian Fellowship Publishers, Inc., 1968), three volumes. Using this understanding of what it means to be a human being, let us look at two areas of importance in appreciating the effect that inner healing can have on our spiritual growth.

Physical Healing and Inner Healing

Because the body, mind, and spirit are all one within each human person, what happens in one part affects the other parts as well. For example, the field of psychosomatic medicine is helping us to see more clearly how our bodies can be made sick and can be made well by what happens in our minds. Similarly, the life that is or is not in our spirits greatly affects how our minds and bodies function. This is one reason that Jesus stated so clearly, "I have come that they may have life and have it to the full" (Jn 10:10).

Spiritual growth through inner healing, then, naturally leads us to living healthier lives. It has led many to see the importance of, as well as giving them divine assistance in, altering their diets, including exercise in their weekly schedule, giving up smoking and drinking altogether or, at least, to excess, and becoming more sensitive to their very real needs for rest, relaxation, and contemplative prayer. In each of the cases that I have witnessed (my own life included), the people involved have experienced a slow but dramatic improvement in the quality of their living. They have more energy, more zest for living; their bodies perform and feel better; they are less prone than they were in the past to colds and diseases; and they function with greater spiritual power.

Similarly, inner healing has brought about cures for physical illnesses. Since many of our physical illnesses are in part caused by psychological and spiritual pain, when this pain is healed through inner healing prayer the physical problems often disappear. I am reminded of a dear friend who was diagnosed by her doctor as having both Parkinson's disease and diabetes; after we prayed about her worries for several members of her family and she gave up trying to solve all their problems, allowing God to bear that responsibility, she returned to her doctor only to find that the Parkinson's disease had disappeared entirely and the diabetes had become so slight it could be controlled by diet.

Yet we must be careful not to presume that every physical

disease has its roots in our psyches or spirits. Some physical diseases are merely physical and need the attention of a competent physician and the love of Jesus mediated through prayer for physical healing. We do need, however, to be aware of the strong correlation between physical and inner healing, and between physical and inner suffering.

For often when we are sick it is a sign from deep within us that something in our minds or in our spirits needs attention—a sign that we need to grow—and when we do that which our inner selves need, we are healed. Some of us will stop long enough to look at our inner selves only when we are physically ill—only then are we ready to admit our need for change and are we willing to try to change, even though the change may be painful. Inner healing and physical healing are connected, then, in many different ways.

Imagination and Inner Healing

In inner healing prayer we use our spirits and our minds in specific ways to pray. Intuitions come from the Holy Spirit into our spirits and find expression through our imagination. If we try to express these intuitions using only our intellects our prayer will be rational and somewhat dry. This is not to say that intellect is an inferior function of our minds, but only that it is not as useful in this kind of praying as imagination is. Imagination makes our prayer come alive, for imagination is the creative function within us, the function that arranges in new ways things given to it by the other parts of our minds and spirits.

Many people do not realize that ordinary people use imagination every day: It is a necessary part of living. Because some people were labeled in school as "unimaginative," "uncreative," and "unartistic" they have been led to believe that imagination is for others but not for them. Others have identified imagination as associated only with things like painting and music and do not see it as a function to be used in everyday life.

But only if we live the dullest of lives do we not use our

imaginations. Many people use their imaginations every day in the ways they approach problems, in the ways they create humor, in the ways they express their feelings, in the ways they reflect on their experiences, in the ways they mend the brokenness they meet in life, and in the ways they pray.

However, we do not all experience our imaginations functioning within us in the same way. Just as personalities vary greatly, so do the imaginations within them. When we begin to understand this fact we will not think less of ourselves for not having the kind of imagination we think we ought to have, and we will learn how to use our own imaginations to give our lives and our prayers more vitality.

For some people imagination operates mainly through concrete pictures, and these people we may identify as having an artistic flair. For others, however, imagination produces abstract ideas that are sometimes related to unclear and indistinct pictures; these may be logical types. A third way that imagination functions within us is in feelings and moods, and people in whom this kind of imagination predominates will be relationship-oriented people and they may find friendships easy to make. And a fourth way that imagination expresses itself is by giving us a sense of the "big picture," by bringing many disparate things together or by seeing the possibilities of things; people who imagine in this way may be visionaries, original thinkers, or individuals who always seem to have a new idea that is just a little "ahead of its time."

In none of us does imagination express itself in only one of these ways; all of us are able to experience two, three, or maybe (if we are very mature) all four of these expressions of imagination functioning regularly within us. But there will be one way in which our imaginations will express themselves most naturally.

It is important to note, then, that none of these ways in which imagination works is better than the others. Each is perfectly valid though of necessity incomplete. When we understand this truth clearly we will not be so ready to judge our prayer, religious experience, or spiritual growth as superior or inferior to that of others; rather, we will see that they are only different, and because of their differences they need the experiences of others to make them complete.

Let it be clear to the reader, therefore, that it is not important to see concrete pictures in one's imagination for inner healing prayer to be successful. However, praying inner healing prayer will help develop whatever type of imagination God has blessed us with. God can work through our imaginations regardless of the way they express themselves—remember, no one kind of imagination is better than the others. I needed to come to this understanding myself because my own imagination is not dominantly concrete, and I must often remind myself that it is just as valid for the imagination to *hear* or to *feel* as it is to *see*.

For example, an inner healing prayer suggests to us to be in the presence of Jesus, Who is smiling at us. We might most naturally *see* this picture in our imaginations. On the other hand, we might *sense* His presence, just as we can sense the presence of another person with us in a room even though we did not see that person enter the room. Or we might *feel* that warm feeling inside that we have had in the past when someone important to us smiles at us. Or we might hear His voice.

What is important is that we do, in some way, use our imaginations when we pray for inner healing; for, while we *know about* a thing or person with our intellects, we *directly know* that thing or person with our imaginations. In other words, imagination carries knowledge from abstraction to experience, from the head to the heart, and it is in our hearts that God first touches us for healing and helps us to grow spiritually.

The Approach of This Book

It is my hope, then, that this book will stimulate the imaginations of its readers not only to experience healing as they read the book but also to create new forms of healing prayer once the book is placed on the shelf. I hope that this book will teach by ideas, examples, and experiences some simple ways to find healing for our inner lives. While this is a practical book, in no way should it be used as a "cookbook," that is, as a set of tested recipes that, if followed to the letter, will necessarily bring healing. Rather, in sharing my practical experience with each form of inner healing prayer described in these pages, I hope to stimulate readers to walk confidently in their own experience, developing their own unique ways of praying.

Every once in a while in talking with people I find someone who prays only prayers for inner healing that someone else has written. While it is important to have these written prayers to help us to learn what inner healing prayer is and how it is to be prayed, it is my hope that in reading this book people will become so comfortable with inner healing prayer that they will learn to pray to God their most personal and entirely unique thoughts and feelings in their own words.

People who pray written inner healing prayers verbatim and never strike out on their own remind me of the two house-wives who were attending a class called "Prayer in the Family." One evening the class discussed spontaneous prayer and they decided that a good time of the day to try this kind of praying in the family would be at grace before the evening meal. Early that week one lady called the other on the phone to ask her how her day was going. "Not too well," was the reply she heard; "I haven't done a thing all day long." "What is the problem?" the first lady asked. The other said, "I've been spending the whole day writing my spontaneous prayer for grace tonight."

Inner healing prayer needs to come from the heart—simply, honestly, sincerely. These are the only truly important criteria for a good prayer. Now, each of the ten chapters of this book will teach the reader "how to" pray a different kind of inner healing prayer for spiritual growth. Each chapter contains general principles of the prayer form, a description of the method, an example of how this kind of prayer helped someone, a sample prayer, a study guide, and suggestions for further reading. It is my hope that, as readers use the sample prayers, they will not only read and pray them but will also *study* them in conjunction with the principles describing the prayer and discover how they can pray this kind of prayer in their own words.

A Note on Using the Sample Prayers in This Book

The sample prayers should be prayed slowly and prayerfully, with many pauses (e.g., after each paragraph, or when we see a series of three or four periods [. . .]). As we pray these sample prayers, whether we use them verbatim or as a model for constructing personal prayer, let us use these steps in preparation. First, we sit comfortably, we sit up straight but not rigidly, placing our feet flat on the floor, relaxing our arms, hands, and legs, and taking everything off our laps. Second, we focus our attention on God, maybe by closing our eyes, or by looking at a favorite picture of Jesus, or by looking at a candle flame and thinking about the Lord's Love for us, and so forth. Third, we regulate and slow down our breathing, for this action takes our minds off our bodies and focuses our energies on our minds and spirits where we need them for prayer. Fourth, if distractions come, we do not concentrate on them—especially we do not berate ourselves for having them; we simply let them go as quickly as they came and gently return our concentration to the Lord and what He is doing for us in prayer.

Now we are ready to learn how to pray for spiritual growth.

Study Guide

1. Can you recognize a time in your life when you experienced healing of your inner self? What was the experience? What were your thoughts and attitudes? What were your feelings?
2. What is your present attitude toward inner healing?
3. How do you feel about the possibility of needing to grow spiritually?
4. What are your attitudes about psychology and its relationship to spiritual growth?
5. In what manner does your imagination function most of the time? Do you think your imagination is free or bound? Give a reason for your answer.

6. What have been your experiences using imagination in prayer? How did these experiences make you feel?

Suggested Reading

Baars, Conrad W., M.D. *Feeling and Healing Your Emotions.* Plainfield, NJ: Logos International, 1979.

Dobson, Theodore E. *Inner Healing: God's Great Assurance.* New York: Paulist Press, 1978.

MacNutt, Francis. *Healing.* Notre Dame, IN: Ave Maria Press, 1974.

Sanford, Agnes. *The Healing Light.* Plainfield, NJ: Logos International, 1978.

Part One

Finding the True Self

Introduction
We Lose Our Lives for Christ to Find Them

"For anyone who wants to save his life will lose it; but anyone who loses his life for my sake will find it" (Mt 16:25).

Jesus and the True Self

"Who am I?" It is a question that is put to every one of us at many stages of our lives, in many different ways. Somehow it is a question that is always there. Even after we have answered it several times, we do not really know the answer, because we are much more complicated than we dare to admit most of the time. We are unknown to ourselves.

"Who is the *real* me?" Every time we answer the question of identity we understand part of the truth, but not all of it. Part of our answer is untrue, a lie, and we believe it along with the truth. How difficult it is to know, face, and simply accept the truth about ourselves! Our "true selves" evade us, and, if we are to tell the truth, we evade our true selves as well.

Jesus wants us to know the truth about ourselves; He wants us to know our true selves, a notion I first learned from Leanne Payne in her book *Real Presence*. Jesus is a lover of the Truth. "Then you will learn the truth and the truth will make you free" (Jn 8:32). He wants us to be filled with life. "I came so that they may have life and have it to the full" (Jn 10:10). And He knows how we can find that life. "For anyone who wants to save his life will lose it; but anyone who loses his life for my sake will find it" (Mt 16:25).

But unfortunately, Christians throughout the ages have often misinterpreted Jesus' words to mean that we must never express who we really are, our true selves. A part of the Christian tradition has taken this verse and several like it about dying to self (e.g., Gal 2:20 and Col 3:10) and used them as a justification for not growing spiritually and finding our true selves at all. The point of what Jesus is saying in Mt 16:25 is that by following His way we ultimately *will* find our true selves. Because we human beings have a natural fear of that Truth, however—a fear based in lies we have believed about ourselves, but a real fear nonetheless—and because it is often difficult and painful to search for that Truth, we have all too easily found in Jesus' words an excuse to avoid all that fear and effort and pain. And in our fear we refuse to reconcile our conclusion with the total Gospel, the Gospel that tells us that Jesus wants us to have abundant life and to know the Truth that will set us free.

How sad—for us and for the world. It is sad for us because we never find out who we are, and because we think Jesus asked us not to, and so we mistakenly think that by living this way we are the essence of Gospel-people. And it is sad for the world, because the world looks at us and says (in a certain sense, rightfully so), "If that is what it means to live as a Christian, I don't want it!" For all they see are people who do not know who they are and therefore cannot be real people or make a significant contribution to life. They see people who look as if they were the "living dead" emotionally and spiritually, and who are proclaiming that the Gospel has done this to them.

Christians who live this way cannot have much energy for service or for spreading the Good News, because most of their energy is unavailable to them. For the essence of life itself, spiritual life, abides in our new selves, which God gives in Baptism, and so if we are not in touch with our true selves we are not in touch with the principle of life within. Such Christians have only enough psychic and spiritual energy then, to make their way through each day. They think that their energy is being sapped by the difficulty of living their faith, but the truth is that they have little energy because they are *not* living according to the *totality* of the faith that Jesus taught.

This is not the way to effect God's will in our lives. Jesus points the way down the path of spiritual growth and self-discovery. He asks only that He can come along, for He knows that the way is dark and only He has enough Light to guide us unerringly on that road. This is one place where Christianity and psychology both meet and diverge. Like psychology, Jesus asks us to find our true selves; but unlike psychology, He does not require us to discover who we really are on our own. On the contrary, He knows that task would be impossible, because our true selves are hidden with Christ in God (Col 3:3); therefore, Jesus—and only Jesus—can successfully lead us to find our true selves.

Self-discovery without Jesus' guiding is introspection, and it easily leads to self-centeredness, pride, confusion, and error. Self-discovery *with* Jesus as guide is inner healing, and when we allow Him to guide every step it leads to God-centeredness, hope, freedom, and joy. This kind of spiritual growth is God's will for us.

Nurturing the False Self

If we are to die to ourselves, it is our false selves to which we must die. Our false selves are all those patterns of thinking, feeling, and behaving that betray in us a false notion of who we are—selfishness, pride, lust, confusion, and the like. Each of us is created in the hand of God as a person who can be actualized only by love in both affirmation and discipline. When we have not been able to find ourselves because we have not been loved, we have been forced to think of ourselves as "something"—that is, as some particular kind of person—and so we identified with false notions of who we are. This identity process often happens at an early age—before six, the psychologists tell us—and this is the reason it is so important that little children are loved and told in word and action that they are lovable. If we are convinced of our lovability in these formative years, we will be able to spend the rest of our lives discovering our true selves and using our potential to contribute to life. But, to the extent to which we were taught we were unlovable, we now have a false self that Jesus wants to—and needs to—heal.

Our false selves have also been nurtured in our adolescence and adulthood by certain brands of spirituality; not all spirituality leads to spiritual growth, and only that which is totally centered in Jesus can bring us into the truth and help us discover our true selves. As we have seen earlier, our fears, laziness, and lack of courage can provide rather strong psychological barriers to our desire to discover the truth and to follow Jesus. Often we have been easily fooled by spiritualities that tell us we do not have to find our true selves.

One of these spiritualities, for example, says that if we do something well, humility demands that we never do that thing. Thinking realistically, however, we know that if humility means acknowledging the truth about ourselves, it means that we acknowledge this capability, and that we also go further and accept the whole truth: that this quality does not originate in ourselves but rather is a gift from the Creator. He who created us in His image calls us to create, that is, to use our gifts and thereby give Him praise, acknowledging that the gift is from Him and giving Him thanks for it. With this attitude we can discover and free our true selves, but—just as important—it is guaranteed that we will remain free, for we are keeping in proper relationship with Him Who is the author of all freedom.

Another spirituality that people have used to excuse themselves from growing spiritually and finding their true selves is to say that God never wants for us what we want for ourselves, our heart's desires. When we think this way, however, we are saying that God is against us and not on our side, thus contradicting His own Word (Rom 8:31–32). While it is true that God's ways are higher than our ways, it is also true that in Baptism God writes His law on our hearts (Jer 31:33) and plants within us the desire to live in goodness and truth (Ez 36:27). These are the deepest desires of our hearts. When we choose not to look at our heart's desires, we choose not to look at God's desire for us (cf. Ps 20:4 and 21:2), and we choose not to find our true selves!

Often we are afraid to look at our deepest desires and to admit what they are. Sometimes, because of the way our society programs us and tries to influence our ways of thinking consciously and unconsciously, some of us fear that our deepest desires will be for something shameful, like promiscuous sexual relations. But in none of us is unlimited sex our deepest desire. Maybe love is. Maybe we desire to give love, to receive love. There are so few ways to express love and affection and sex is one of them, so human beings have often confused the desire for sex with the desire for love. It seems that this is true of our society in general. But if we look deep within ourselves for our heart's desire we will not find something that would shame us; rather, we will find the traces of God's handiwork in creating us. Do we believe that we are made in His very image and likeness?

More deeply than anything else we desire integrity, wholeness, and to be able to contribute to life. Each person needs, however, to discover in what specific way he desires these things. We may have other desires that are less laudable, but they are not our deepest desires. When we allow these secondary desires to prevent us from finding our heart's desire, we nurture our false selves, and simultaneously we put to death our true selves! This is not Christ's way.

Christ Discovers Our True Selves

Through inner healing Jesus discovers our true selves. This is a joyous experience, for the false self dies. It is when people see Christians putting to death their true selves that "death to self" becomes repugnant to them. And it should, under these circumstances! For when Christians put their true selves to death, while many of them are motivated by the highest goals, they are not following the teachings of Jesus. Their lives may be very religious, but they are not living the way of spiritual growth, the unique view of life Jesus taught and lived.

All through the ages, the great saints who have gone before us, our spiritual parents, have witnessed to the biblical truth that God has made us to give Him praise by being the persons we are. As St. Irenaeus (died ca. 203) said, "The glory of God is a human being fully alive."

Again, we see the difference between that to which Jesus calls us and that to which totally humanistic self-realization calls us. Inner healing and spiritual growth are not *self*-realization: they are not self finding self, for that is an impossibility. Inner healing is Jesus finding our true selves; it is Jesus-centered.

Paul said it this way: "Make sure that no one traps you and deprives you of your freedom through some secondhand, empty, rational philosophy based on the principles of this world instead of on Christ. In his body lives the fullness of divinity, and in him you too find your own fulfillment, in the One Who is head of every Sovereignty and Power" (Col 2:8–9). Therefore, we do not want to follow, for example, psychology alone; rather, we want to follow Christ, Who has the divine nature to give to us, Who can deal with every power over our lives—physical, psychological, and spiritual—and with every worldly value that claims authority over us, for example, money, sex, pride, selfishness, and bitterness.

When we entered Christ, Paul continues, we came into full life, for life is not only physical but also of the spirit. All that was opposed to our life and growth He took away and nailed to the Cross, forever disarming those powers from having authority over us (Col 2:11–15). They remain powerless over us as we remain in Christ. But when we leave Christ and completely entrust our lives to something of merely human origins like humanism, psychology, ideologies, materialism, or just the contemporary mores of modern society, those "empty and rational philosophies" can have power over us again. This is not to say that everything in psychology, philosophy, humanism, and so forth, is empty. There is much, much good in them. What is dangerous is putting them in the center—making Jesus' teaching conform to psychology, or evaluating Jesus' teaching by the standards of philosophical teaching. Rather, we evaluate human wisdom by the way in which it agrees with Jesus' teaching. Jesus is the norm, not worldly wisdom.

Once we live in this biblical point of view we can use whatever of secular sciences and philosophies comes our way and agrees with Jesus in order to free our true selves. Doing so creates in us a God-consciousness centered in Jesus, and this is the essence of praise—to be as fully conscious of God as we can, because our true selves have been liberated by Jesus, Whom we have invited to live in the center of our beings. Freeing our true selves to praise God with all that we have and are is the first goal of spiritual growth through inner healing.

Praying to Find Our True Selves

We will look at four kinds of prayer through which we can discover the true self within each of us. These, however, are not all the possible ways to pray to discover the true self. It is my hope that these chapters will stimulate the reader's imagination to find even more ways to pray for this freedom, at the very least, to develop his own way to pray these prayers, putting them into his own words.

The four ways of praying are these: cleansing the imagination, intellect, and will; silence and listening to God; journal-keeping; and integrating and balancing opposites.

Study Guide

1. Describe the "real you," as much as you are able to do so.
2. What are some of the ideas you have believed that have prevented you from finding your true self and have nurtured your false self?
3. What are the deepest desires of your heart? (Answer only after a period of silent reflection on this question.)

4. What are the signs by which you can tell that you do or do
   not live by Paul's words: "Therefore, there is now no condemnation for those who are in Christ Jesus" (Rom 8:1 NIV)?
5. What do you understand St. Irenaeus to mean when he said,
   "The glory of God is a human being fully alive"?

Suggested Reading

Baars, Conrad W., M.D. *Feeling and Healing Your Emotions.*
     Plainfield, NJ: Logos International, 1979.
————, and Terruwe, Anna A., M.D. *Healing the Unaffirmed.*
     New York: Alba House, 1976.
Finley, James. *Merton's Palace of Nowhere: A Search for God through
     Awareness of the True Self.* Notre Dame, IN: Ave Maria
     Press, 1978.
Lewis, C. S. *The Great Divorce.* New York: Macmillan Publish-
     ing Co., Inc., 1976.
Payne, R. Leanne. *Real Presence: The Holy Spirit in the Works of C.
     S. Lewis.* Westchester, IL: Cornerstone Books, 1979.
Tapscott, Betty. *The Fruit of the Spirit.* Houston, TX: Hunter
     Books, 1978.

Chapter 1
Cleansing the Imagination, Intellect, and Will

Imagination, intellect, will, and memory comprise our minds or psyches. Each of these functions is given to us by God to reflect or image a part of Him (Gn 1:27) and each is supposed to do something unique and good within us according to God's plan. However, each part of us was darkened by sin in the Fall of Adam and Eve; and so the imagination, intellect, will, and memory are darkened and lead us into the darkness of the false self until they are consecrated to God. They on their own can discover and cling to nothing of eternal value, nothing of all the important things for which mankind longs; we must be reborn in Jesus for our minds to enter the Kingdom of God (cf. Jn 3:5).

It was in His understanding of this truth that Jesus said, "I am the Way, the Truth, and the Life. No one comes to the Father except through me" (Jn 14:6). He is the Way that redeems our wills, the Truth that redeems our intellects, and the Life that redeems our imaginations, so that, filled with Jesus, we can find our true selves and come to the Father, Who is the goal of our lives.

It is important, then, to learn how to fill each of these functions of our minds with Jesus as a first step in our spiritual growth. We need Jesus to consecrate them to God and to cleanse them of all the unholy things with which we have filled them. Thus given to God and filled with God they can be used without fear that they will lead us astray. Rather, we can trust them, not because they in themselves are powerful or wonderful, but because they are consecrated and guided by Jesus through His Spirit.

And so this chapter comes first in learning how to pray for spiritual growth, because until we cleanse and dedicate our minds we will have a difficult time using them in inner healing prayer. However, for the sake of simplicity, from this point on we will speak only of cleansing the imagination, trusting that the reader will apply what is said to each of the functions within our minds.

General Principles

When an image comes into our imaginations that we judge to be wrong, immoral, or evil, we have been well schooled in the ways of the world to repress that image, to feel guilty, and to call ourselves evil for having it. By repressing the image, however, we do not rid ourselves of it; on the contrary, we store it away in our unconscious minds. There it becomes a part of our false selves, a part of the way we view the world and ourselves, a part of our motivation for future actions.

For example, one day when I am daydreaming a thought comes into my mind of how I could get back at a person who has hurt me; when I become conscious of the fact that I am thinking vengeful and bitter thoughts I become ashamed of myself and say, "This is terrible! I shouldn't be thinking this way. These thoughts are un-Christian, so I must stop thinking this way and put these thoughts out of my mind."

Now, we know that we are in trouble when we start to use words like "should" and "ought" and "must," because these words are signs that we are at war with ourselves. If we are at war within we do not have peace, and where there is not peace neither Jesus nor His Spirit can abide. If we succeed in repressing the thought, we also repress the tension of this struggle, only for it to reappear at a later time in some action that will relieve the tension and express the thought; that action will be sin. Under the guise of doing something good and Christian, then, we are really doing great harm to ourselves; for the Bible does not say that we are to put evil thoughts out of our conscious minds and repress them into our unconscious (thus adding to our false selves); it says that we are to put unconstructive and evil thoughts away and get rid of them entirely—namely, in Eph 4:31 and Col 3:5–8—thus freeing our true selves.

How can we do that? The simple answer is that we cannot! Unassisted we have no power to extract any images out of our own minds. Unassisted we are doomed either to repress or to think about any images that come to us. The answer to our dilemma is in Jesus. "Let the peace of Christ rule in your hearts" (Col 3:15)—this is the only solution to our problem. Jesus' approach must be ours if we are to be freed of the thoughts and feelings that we find in ourselves that keep us from growing.

How does Christ bring peace into our hearts? First He asks us to be open and honest about our thoughts. Whenever Jesus met evil and destructiveness He had the same approach: "Repent of your sin and I will forgive." We cannot repent of our sin, of the evil of our false selves, if we do not acknowledge it is there. We cannot repent of our sin, similarly, if we only think about it and do not tell anyone of it. Repentance means honesty and confession.

So, rather than condemning ourselves for the bitter thought of revenge that we were thinking, Jesus calls us honestly and freely to bring it to Him to begin the process of spiritual growth "There is now no condemnation for those who are in Christ Jesus" (Rom 8:1 NIV). By entering relationship with Jesus, we can avoid condemning ourselves and being condemned. When we are honest with the Lord about our bitter thoughts we are giving Him the opportunity to cleanse our imaginations of the images of revenge that are controlling them, and so we have the opportunity to discover our true selves.

Jesus knows that we have thoughts of vengeance, violence, lust, pride; there is no sense in trying to hide from Him what He already knows. And yet that is what we try to do when we repress our evil thoughts—we are trying to hide them from Him and from ourselves. We do not want to admit that such a thought could come from us. We are afraid to admit that we have the potential for evil. However, if we lose touch with our potential for evil, two dire consequences await us: Our potential for evil will be out of the control of our conscious minds and therefore it will be more apt to be in control of us; and we will also lose touch with our potential for good. In other words, we will not know who we are.

It seems that there are many people in our society who are in this state today. Because they justify their evil thoughts and rationalize their evil deeds, they also cannot see clearly the good within themselves. Therefore, they are ripe for the evil repressed in their unconscious minds to rise up and take over their lives. They live lives of mutual destruction in hatred, anger, jealousy, and the like and create fruitless and frustrating relationships. Our newspapers are filled with their stories, our social agencies are backed up with their cases, and our courts are logjammed with their litigations.

Jesus' answer to all this is that we need not fear our potential for evil if we immediately bring it to Him, for He has been victorious over all evil. Because of His Cross, none of us on earth needs to be in bondage to the evil of which we are capable. Therefore, Jesus asks us to tell Him the thoughts of our minds and to let them go into His hands, thereby cleansing our inner selves and making us whole and wholesome.

This would seem to be a simple procedure except for one other hurdle: our desire to enjoy the evil our minds concoct. Sometimes we neither want to repress our evil thoughts nor to give them up; we want to concentrate on them and enjoy them. Consequently, one person can enjoy plotting how he will bring vengeance on his enemy, and another person may enjoy her lustful thoughts, and another person may enjoy another's bad fortune.

Therefore, after we are ready to admit honestly our evil before Jesus, one thing more is required—to desire to be rid of it. Even this desire, however, is a gift. Just as we cannot heal ourselves or change ourselves in any permanent way, neither can we *desire* to do so on our own. This desire comes from God.

"It is God, for his own loving purpose, who puts the will and
the action into you" (Phil 2:13).

All we can do on our own, then, is to desire the desire. The
rest is God's work. What a comfort to know how little relies on
our own capabilities! Though small, however, this is still a great
challenge; it is about as much as human beings can handle. But
we can handle it; it is not outside our grasp. It is good to know
that God does not ask the impossible or the unusually difficult;
He asks of us only what we can do, and He promises to do the
rest in the process of our spiritual growth.

A Description of the Prayer

First, then, we need to admit that our imaginations need
cleansing, that they are filled with all kinds of images that do us
no good whatsoever and that often lead us into spiritual destruction instead of into spiritual growth. And second, we need to
want to let go of those images. We need to be able to approach
Jesus and say honestly and simply, "I do not desire these
thoughts nor do I desire the pleasure I have in the past derived
from them. The pleasure I desire is You, and the thoughts and
images I want for my imagination are Your thoughts and images. Then I will be happy as You are happy, for I will be living
in my true self."

But if we cannot honestly say these things, all is not lost!
We do not need to turn away until we have collected enough
courage to give up these images. Rather, we turn even this
situation into a prayer. Since all desires for good things are
themselves gifts from God (Phil 2:13) we pray for the *desire* to
admit that our imaginations need cleansing, we pray for the
desire to let go of these former sources of illicit pleasure—
pleasure that has hurt us much more than helped us. No matter
what inner state in which we find ourselves in life, we can use
that state as a springboard to prayer just by turning to God,
Who is happy to accept us in the state in which we find
ourselves.

And what prayer would God want to answer more than a prayer to desire to discover our true selves? This is a prayer He will not refuse, for in no way is it selfish nor will it bring us to harm. God will begin to answer this prayer by slowly but perceptibly changing our thoughts about what is pleasurable and what is not, and about who we are and who we are not, so that in time we come to see things from His point of view, and we desire what He desires for us.

When we are ready to admit our thoughts to Him, and when we are ready to let them go and no longer desire the pleasure they yield, we stand in the presence of Jesus and invite Him to send His Holy Spirit into the depth of our imaginations, to stir up every image of wrongdoing and evil, and to bring them into our conscious minds. This would be a dangerous exercise if we were not doing it in the presence of Jesus; but when we are with Him the brightness of His Light reveals the truth about these thoughts, and we are no longer duped by the glamour they once held for us.

As the images come into our conscious minds, then, we continue to see Jesus in front of us or to sense His presence in some way. We see Him standing with His hands outstretched, waiting for us to put our thoughts into His hands. As each thought comes into our conscious minds, we pluck it from our minds and, placing it in His hands, see what He does with it. It is helpful for many people to make this "giving up" more real by going through the physical motion of bringing the hand to the forehead, "holding" the thought in the fingers, and reaching forward placing the thought into Jesus' cupped hands. When we act the prayer out in this way, it helps to actualize our desires to renounce these images of evil.

As we place the image in Jesus' hands, we watch what He does with it, for He does not only want to take it away. Our minds were never meant to have those kinds of thoughts in them, and so Jesus will want either to transform the thought in some way into something good so that He can then give it back to us, or He will want to replace it with something else that is good and wholesome, like His Light or His Love, so as to heal the wound it has made in our imaginations. We need to see or to feel how Jesus heals us uniquely.

We repeat this action over and over again with every thought that comes into our conscious minds. Remember, we have invited the Spirit to stir up *every* image that we have ever stored in our minds. Therefore, this prayer often takes much longer than we would at first suspect, for images come out of us that we have long ago repressed and forgotten; yet they have still been there affecting the ways we think, feel, and behave. But with this prayer we are freeing our true selves of them. Therefore, as each image comes forward we place it in Jesus' hands and see what He does with it. For various reasons, some people find it necessary to pray this prayer several times to stir up and deal with all the images in their minds.

When the imagination is cleansed we can dedicate it to God by seeing it as something concrete like a stone connected to us by cords. We take the stone into our hands and then give it to Jesus, cutting the cords (our attachment to our imaginations— i.e., our desires to do whatever we want with them) and allowing Jesus to hold and to own our imaginations. By having this total authority over our imaginations, He can make them holy. This may be a difficult and painful prayer to pray, because in it we may for the first time recognize how much we have held on to or prized our imaginations as our own possessions, and because, as we give them to Jesus, we may see in what terrible condition our imaginations are, for we have not had the wisdom to know how to care for them. But whatever pain comes will be a healing pain, and the tears healing tears, for through this experience we will be giving ourselves in a real way to God.

If after we pray this prayer some of these thoughts return to our minds again, this is not a cause for alarm. We need to remember that we have ingrained many of these thoughts in our minds for years and years, so that one decision and prayer may not be able to put them to rest. At these times we draw on the power of the desire that God has placed in us to be rid of these thoughts and again we place them in Jesus' hands. After some persistence even these ingrained thoughts will leave, not to be remembered, never again to control our imaginations and all that comes from them.

An Example

It was my dear friend Leanne Payne, author and gifted lay minister of healing, who taught me this prayer, first by praying it with me. At that time in my life, I had realized that certain images of vengeance had been with me for much of my life, some of them from early childhood. With these images, I constructed a fantasy world into which I fled when I needed to feel superior to others, thus allowing my false self to take over my personality. On realizing that these images had controlled my thinking for a long time, I began to grow disgusted with them and I wanted to be rid of them. I dealt with the issue of receiving pleasure from them as honestly as I could—I did not immediately say I wanted to be rid of these images, but I recognized that, while a certain part of me was repelled by them, another part of me was attracted to them. And after praying about this situation for a while, I decided that, even though it would be painful to give up this source of pleasure, whatever Jesus had in store for me would be better than the degradation into which these images brought me whenever they took over my mind.

And so I decided to desire to be rid of them all—not to hold on to one of them. Leanne prayed with me to strengthen this resolve, for it is through this decision that the Lord is free to work as He wills in the imagination. Then she asked me to pray with her to invite the Holy Spirit deep within my imagination to bring into consciousness every one of these images. One by one they came forward; some were all too familiar, others I remembered as images I had toyed with many years ago but had long forgotten. All of them came forward, for Jesus wanted to clean out from my imagination all the junk that I had put into it.

As each thought came forward, I reached up to my head with my hands and "plucked" it from my mind with my fingers and placed it in the hands of Jesus, Whom I imagined standing before me with His hands cupped and waiting. As I gave each thought to Jesus He dropped it into the pits of hell. There was no fear that these thoughts would tempt me to sin at this time, for when I saw them in the presence of Jesus I saw how ugly they were, and they were not attractive to me. After Jesus disposed of each ugly thought, He placed His hands glowing with soft Light on my forehead, and Light filled the space where each of the ugly thoughts had been.

During the following two weeks some of these thoughts returned. At this point my faith in what I clearly felt Jesus had done was tested. I decided that while the healing had been real, there was another reality with which to contend, namely, that I had ingrained these images in my imagination by years of repetition. It was no wonder that they did not go away with one decision and one prayer!

So, when they came back, I again gave them to Jesus. I did this before I could even think about them or be tempted by them—a sign that the first prayer had already taken effect to some degree. I quickly followed the same format of praying that Leanne had taught me and I let the thoughts go.

None of these images now remains within me. I cannot even remember what they were. When my thinking goes down paths that would have in the past come to rest in these images, my mind now averts those paths on its own. For my imagination is now the Lord's and because He owns it, fills it, and cares for it, it has many desires other than sinful ones—desire to know the truth, to create beauty, and to pray (this is how the true self functions).

I find now that I have more control over my imagination. I find, too, that I am inclined to pray much more than I was before Leanne ministered to me in this way. While my imagination can still invent new images that would lead me into sin and sometimes does, I no longer feel helpless when this happens. I know that if I decide to give the thought to Jesus He will take care of it. That decision became easier for me to make after I used this method of prayer to cleanse my will of all the effects of the decisions for evil that I had made in my life.

A Sample Prayer

Before we begin to pray this prayer, let us turn back for a moment to the very last section of the Preface and review the four steps that will help us prepare to pray. They are in the section entitled "A Note on Using the Sample Prayers in This Book." Once we have taken the time to complete these simple preparations we can begin to pray.

"Jesus, thank You for the chance to come to You in prayer and ask You to find my true self. Thank You for being so caring of every part of me, of every detail of my life. Thank You for this time that we have together. I ask You to guide my prayer, and to use this time in whatever way You see as best for me right now.

"Jesus, I come to You with special concern for my imagination, which I confess to You that I have mis-used and filled with all kinds of thoughts and images that have done me harm, that have brought sin into my life. Lord, I know only in part what I have done; for only You see all the effects that my decisions have had on my life, only You see how the contents of my imagination have formed and directed my life—often for the worse. But, Lord, even though I don't see all that I could, I am sorry. Please forgive me. Show me how to pray today to be freed of the sinful thoughts and images in my imagination.

"I know, Jesus, that there is a part of me that wants to give up all these evil thoughts so that I can grow spiritually, but there is another part of me that enjoys them. I am not of one mind on this matter. Only You, Jesus, can resolve my double-mindedness. Jesus, I cannot honestly say that on my own I can give up these thoughts and the pleasure that comes with them; I cannot even say that I desire to give them up. But I can say that I desire to desire to give them up. Thank You, Jesus, that this is all You require of me, for it is difficult enough. I trust that, if You free me of these thoughts,

*You will replace them with something that will be
even more comforting and pleasurable in a holy way. I
see myself as being simpler, happier, and freer if I
allow You to have Your way in my imagination. So let
it be. I desire the desire to be freed of all the evil
thoughts and images within me."*

It could be that, for a certain time, this will be as far as we
can pray this prayer honestly. If that is so, it is fine. We can rest
in the fact that Jesus loves us just as we are, and that in His love
He will answer our prayer in time. Until, however, we actually
experience the grace of the desire to be free of all these thoughts
and images, it would be best not to continue this prayer, for that
would be dishonest and therefore fruitless. So we wait with the
Lord, and in His time we will have what we desire. If, however,
that desire is truly in our hearts, we can continue to pray.

*"Therefore, Lord, I ask You to send Your Holy Spirit
deep within me into my conscious and unconscious
mind, into my imagination, and I give Him permission
to release from within me every image of vengeance,
violence, jealousy, lust, pride, and whatever else may
occupy my imagination with evil intentions. As these
images come to the forefront of my mind, I will give
them to You, Jesus, and ask You to deal with them as
You see fit, and to heal that part of my imagination that
has been harmed by harboring these thoughts."*

At this point we wait until the images come forth. As each
one comes into our consciousness, we pluck it from our minds
and place it in the hands of Jesus, Who is standing before us. It
will be helpful for many of us to go through the physical motion
of plucking the thought from our minds. As we place the image
in Jesus' hands, we watch to see what He does with it. This is
most important, for it is the completion of the healing of our
imaginations traumatized by evil images they were never made
to contain.

We repeat this action over and over again until every

thought and image is cleansed from us. This may take more time than we at first anticipate because of the number of repressed images that may come forth. As this process is continuing we can pray simple prayers to Jesus, thanking Him for what is happening. When we sense that all the images have been dealt with, we can continue and conclude the prayer.

> *"Now, Jesus, You have cleansed my imagination. It is Yours. I give it to You. I imagine it as something concrete, something I can hold in my hands. I see that it is connected to me by cords with names like vanity, possessiveness, and pride. Let me place my imagination in Your hands. Jesus, sever these cords with the sword of Your Spirit. I give You permission to sever each one of them."*

We take the time to imagine this scene and to feel the sense of loss, just as if we had just given away the most prized possession of our lives.

> *"I see, Lord, as I give my imagination to You, that what I clung to so completely is rather ugly and not in the best of condition. It has been corroded from within by my misuse of it. I will entrust it to You to fill it with desires for goodness, with creativity, with a sense of wonder, and with a caring for all creation. I will trust You to lead me through my imagination to understand all that is Real about life and love. I will trust You to find my true self.*
>
> *"Thank You, Jesus, for the freedom You give me today. Thank You for making me new and innocent again. Teach me to look to You again and again when my imagination needs to be purified because of the influence of the world or because of the evil within me. I appreciate what You have done to help me grow spiritually. I love You, Jesus. Show me how to love You ever more completely. Amen."*

Study Guide

1. What are the signs you can see that your own imagination needs to be cleansed and dedicated to God? Your intellect? Your will?
2. What is the difference between repressing something into the unconscious mind and getting rid of it entirely?
3. How does total honesty lead to repentance?
4. What are the signs in your life that you are out of touch with the good and/or evil that you can do?
5. Describe a time in which you came to desire what God wanted for you more than you desired what you wanted for yourself.

Suggested Reading

Baars, Conrad W., M.D. *Feeling and Healing Your Emotions.* Plainfield, NJ: Logos International, 1979.

Payne, R. Leanne. *Real Presence: The Holy Spirit in the Works of C. S. Lewis.* Westchester, IL: Cornerstone Books, 1979.

Sanford, John. *The Kingdom Within.* Ramsey, NJ: Paulist Press, 1980.

Chapter 2
The Prayer of Quiet
and Listening to God

Most people discover how to listen to God through a practical question or a pressing personal experience: People want to know how to pray for healing, or they need some specific guidance in their lives, or they become tired of personal prayer in which they do all the talking and never seem to receive a response. Each of these situations brings up the topic of spiritual growth through listening to God, for listening to God is the only answer to these questions and the only solution to these problems.

Let us take as an example a situation in which we want to know for what we should pray when we are praying for healing for ourselves. How do we *know* what should be the focus of our prayer? There is only one answer: We must ask God what He wants done and then listen for His answer; then we pray for that which He suggests. For, if we want our prayers to succeed, we cannot merely pray for whatever seems best to us. Daily, Christians pray the words, "Your will be done, on earth as it is in heaven." But if we are really praying for *our* will to be done, we have in our own minds deposed God and taken His place. Also, if we pray for our will to be done, we are not sure our prayer can or even ought to be answered; for only what God wants *will* be done. Only He sees the total picture and knows exactly the best thing to do at any moment.

We must pray, then, for *God's* will to be done; and to find out what He wants, we must ask Him. But another question quickly arises: When we ask God to reveal His will and we hear an answer within us, how do we know whether we have heard God's voice? Could this not be our own thought?

Yes, it could. And that is the reason that the second chapter of this book addresses the topic of how to listen for God's voice. It is most important for Christians to be able to distinguish God's voice from the many other voices of self within, especially if we want to learn how to pray for our own spiritual growth and inner healing.

General Principles

The ancient teaching of Christianity is that, through the Holy Spirit and His gifts of faith, hope, and love, Jesus Christ lives within every Christian. Paul taught this truth many times, for example," I live now not with my own life but with the life of Christ who lives in me" (Gal 2:20).

If Jesus is living within each of us, He is there purposefully. One reason He lives within us is so that we can be close to Him and He to us. Our closeness is not a purely emotional thing—although it does have many strong emotions involved in it—but it is also practical. Christ's indwelling is His way of being our guide, friend, and Lord. We do not have to go far to find Him or to discover His will so that we can do it; we only have to listen within for His voice.

Therefore, we know that Jesus lives within each of us and speaks to us all the time. We do not hear His voice as an audible experience, but rather as an inner voice comparable to the thoughts in our minds. An important part of the *nature* of a Christian, an important part of the *new nature* that Jesus gives to us in Baptism (Rom 6:1–11), is being in constant communion with Christ within us. When we listen to Him and follow His way, we become His friends. Sin breaks off this communication, and a Spirit-filled Christian life opens it up.

When we sin, what have we done except allow our own will to override Jesus' will for us? Sin, therefore, immerses us in self, that is, in our old selves and our false selves. When these selves rule us, our views of ourselves, the world, and God become distorted and disoriented, and spiritual growth becomes difficult, if not impossible. All the different voices within us begin to fight for a chance to be heard. There is the child's voice, the voice of the law-giver, the practical voice; there is a guilty voice, an optimistic voice, a fearful voice; there is the voice of the trickster, the voice of wisdom, the voice of selfishness; and the list could go on and on. All of these voices are parts of our personalities, but sometimes they function on their own as well, and they speak to us when we do not ask them to do so.

When we sin, we remove from their midst the only master that has the authority to take charge of them all—Jesus. Only He can bring direction to the inner self. Through sin, the false self tries to assert leadership, but because that self has no real authority, it is quickly overthrown by one after another of these voices. No wonder that when we look within we often become afraid and confused, and we want to run away!

This is one of the chief effects of sin in our lives: fear of self and fear of the spiritual world we can find within. Even if we have given our lives to Jesus and we know that He has forgiven our sins, we still need to grapple with this *effect* that our sins have in us. We are out of order within, and this is the reason that we cannot hear God clearly when He speaks to us.

How, then, do we reassert our proper Christian natures, which Christ has given us in Baptism? How do we learn to let God's voice reign once again within us? How do we quiet all the other voices within and teach them to speak only when they are needed?

We can learn the prayer of quiet. We can learn how to seek God's voice within and, when we pray, how not to pay attention to all those other voices that fight for our attention. We can learn how we can gently break down the power of distractions and focus our entire selves on Jesus, Who lives within.

We began this investigation by asking how we can hear God's voice when we are praying for healing for ourselves. One thing we know with surety is that we will never be able to hear

God's voice when we are praying for healing if we cannot first hear His voice in our daily conversational prayer. For when we are asking God for healing we are under pressure: We need to hear God's voice *now* on some *specific* matter. And we know that we never work as well under that kind of pressure as we do when we are relaxed. Therefore, if we want to hear God's guidance in our healing prayers, we first need to seek His voice in our daily prayer when the situation is relaxed and it is not so important whether we make a mistake or succeed.

A Description of the Prayer

Jesus will speak to each of us in a different way, because each of us is unique. That means tht it is useless to feel superior or inferior to another person because of the manner in which Jesus and that person communicate. All that is important is that all of us find our own way of listening to the Lord and become familiar with that way.

When we pray the prayer of quiet we will be seeking the voice of God within—not an audible voice. God often speaks in a still, quiet voice, but a voice with a certain firmness and soundness (1 Kings 19:9–18). However He makes Himself known within us, His voice will be noticeably different from all the other voices we hear in our minds.

But discerning His voice at first must be a matter of trial and error. We collect ourselves by praying the prayer of quiet, we ask a question, we concentrate in a relaxed and quiet kind of way, we hear a response. We try to notice the "tone" of the voice of the response and remember it. We do what we have heard. If what we have done proves to be right, true, and good, we have heard God's voice within, and when we hear that voice again we will listen attentively. If it results in something wrong or harmful we have to listen for another voice.

Often we will know immediately whether the voice we have heard is God's as we compare what is said with Scripture: If the two disagree, the voice we have heard was not from the

Lord. Or if the voice tells us to do something totally ridiculous, harmful, or meaningless, we know that the voice is not from Jesus. If the voice tells us to do something that would violate a well-trained conscience, it is not of God.

The prayer of quiet is of itself the simplest of prayers. First, we allow between twenty and sixty minutes for this prayer; for if we give this prayer less than twenty minutes we will not be able to wade through all of the distractions and come to the time of prayer itself, and more than sixty minutes is too long a time for such concentration unless the Lord specifically leads along those lines.

Second, we become comfortable but we sit upright with all the members of our bodies relaxed; our feet are flat on the floor, our arms and hands are relaxed on our lap or on the arms of a chair, and we loosen the muscles of the neck so that they feel comfortable. We also begin to breathe slowly and regularly. By doing these things we are trying to take attention away from our bodies so that we can fully concentrate in our minds and spirits.

Third, we begin to pray. Our prayer is short, slow, and constantly repeated. Our prayer can be simply one or two words that become as natural as breathing to us: "Abba," "Father," "Jesus," "Lord, have mercy," "Come, Lord Jesus," or any other short prayer that might resonate within us as a prayer we could pray sincerely. Or maybe we use the ancient "Jesus Prayer" of the Eastern Church: "Lord Jesus Christ, Son of God, have mercy upon me, a sinner."

The specific words themselves matter little (non-Christian mantras excluded, of course). What does matter is the one element that all these prayers have in common: They focus our attention entirely outside of ourselves and onto God, with Whom we want to commune. Because this kind of praying is so simple, and because its focus is not on ourselves or on our concerns but on God, the first result of praying in this fashion is that every distraction within us will come into our conscious minds. We will remember a thousand things that we must accomplish; our thoughts will wander to the problems we face;

we will even be distracted by ideas about how we could be more sensitive to a particular person or how we could meet his or her needs.

The fact that these distractions come forward is good! These are precisely the "voices" we hear subliminally all day long, the voices that make such a noise that we cannot hear God. When each of them comes forward we can still it by gently turning away from it (except for the list of things to be done, which we might write down); once again we think about what we are saying, trying to stretch ourselves and reach out to touch God—not that we *will* touch God; but if we reach out for Him long enough He will touch us!

We can see that a more complicated prayer would not have this effect. In discursive prayer, in which we voice to God our feelings, desires, requests, thanksgivings, and praises, we can become lost in the words, or the words themselves may express the confusion of all the voices within us. While this prayer has its own value, it does not pierce through our inner confusion to still the noise and find God's voice.

However, when we pray the prayer of quiet, we need to be ready for the possibility that we will not like it. For some people it can be extremely frustrating (unfortunately for these people, they probably need this kind of prayer the most), for the distractions may seem endless and the time of prayer wasted. While other forms of prayer may have more immediate satisfaction, *nothing* can replace the prayer of quiet for calming our inner selves and finding our true selves, as well as for finding the voice of God within.

Also, it may take many hours of this kind of praying before we break through the wall of confusion that surrounds our true selves and the voice of God. I myself prayed the prayer of quiet and the Jesus Prayer off and on for three years (I prayed twenty minutes a day, three or four days a week, for several weeks in a row; then I became frustrated and angry and gave it up for a few months; finally I came back to try it again only to have a similar experience—in hindsight, however, I saw that each time I came back to the prayer it was a little easier, a little more successful) before I felt that God had broken through and we were finally communicating more directly. And I have discovered that I can lose this communion with God if I give up praying in this way for too long a period of time; then, in a sense, I need to start over.

Once we have broken through the confusion barrier our prayer of quiet can expand in scope into meditation on one line of Scripture, into seeking guidance, into various forms of inner healing prayer, or simply into relaxing with Jesus. At this stage of our development, we use the short repetitive prayer to begin and settle into our true selves and, having disposed of any distractions by simply averting them, we commune with Jesus in whatever way His Spirit may lead.

One problem that some people have in praying this way is that they tend to fall asleep in the middle of the prayer. If we experience this reaction, we should look for the solution in one of several practical areas—to begin with, diet, rest, and a medical checkup. Many who experience this reaction simply are not giving themselves enough time to sleep and they need the rest. Others may be eating incorrectly, ingesting too much sugar, carbohydrates, or red meat. Still others may have a more refined problem that only a doctor could detect.

Sleep, however, may also be a sign of an unresolved conflict with the Lord. I remember when I was in school I often dealt with the pressure of exam week by sleeping my study time away, for I unconsciously knew that any time I spent sleeping I did not have to spend concentrating on my difficult studies. Often we sleep to avoid things that we need to face directly.

If we find ourselves running from the prayer of quiet because of a reaction of revulsion, disinterest, or sleep, it could be that we are running from certain feelings we have toward God that are too threatening for us to face. Maybe we are angry with Him, disappointed in Him, frustrated by Him, fighting for control with Him. Only the Holy Spirit, however, can tell us what our unique problem with this kind of praying is, and so we need to ask Him in prayer and maybe also seek the counsel of some trusted spiritual guide.

An Example

As I mentioned above, in my own prayer life it took years before I could begin to hear God's guidance clearly. Even now I cannot always do it, for hearing God depends on so many variable factors, over some of which I have no control and over others of which I have control but I make the wrong decisions. But as I began to pray the prayer of quiet, I found that I first began to hear God—although at times more vaguely than I would have wished—in my compassion for others in pain as I tried to minister to them and pray healing prayer with them, in my deepest feelings about life and friends, in the words of the Bible, which seemed more and more to speak directly to me, and in the Eucharist.

But the prayer of quiet itself was a frustrating experience for me. I prayed it only sporadically at first, because I did not see any immediate fruit from the time I spent in that kind of prayer. I suppose that I was guided by my feelings more than was good for me, yet the experience of those frustrating years helps me to be compassionate with people in similar straits today.

Most frustrating to me was the fact that I could go only so far and no further down the road into my true self and the presence of God within. I would pray the Jesus Prayer and come to a point at which I sensed that I was in the presence of Jesus, but it was as if there was a mist or a veil between Him and me. I could "see" Him but only dimly, "hear" Him but only faintly, choose to do as He instructed but only sporadically.

What I did not realize then but can see only in hindsight is that this prolonged time of frustration was a signal that there was a deeper unresolved issue between Jesus and me that I had not yet faced squarely. Praying the Jesus Prayer and spending time listening in silence provided a kind of gentle pressure that necessarily pushed me to find a resolution to this problem. So the prayer of quiet was healing for me because it gently forced me to face an important issue that, if left unresolved, would have stunted my spiritual growth indefinitely.

One day in the middle of a directed retreat, the issue that needed facing came forth on its own. This was a moment of grace, and nothing I could ever have done would have made it happen one second sooner. If I could have made it happen sooner, I would not have been able to face it, for when I dealt with this issue I did so with all the spiritual and emotional strength that I had developed in the three years of praying the prayer of quiet.

I had finished my afternoon meditation somewhat early, and was spending the rest of my allotted time praying the Jesus Prayer while sitting in front of a life-sized crucifix. As I prayed, some unusual emotions began stirring inside of me, and it seemed to me best that I allow them to come forward. So I continued to pray the Jesus Prayer, and the feelings grew. In time they became quite strong, possibly because of their shocking nature, definitely because they had been repressed for so long a time.

What I felt was a surging rage, a totally irrational yet quite real anger at Jesus crucified. I ask the reader to remember that I know these feelings were irrational as I describe them, for I am not trying to justify them—they were some of the effects of sin in my life. I was angry with Jesus for dying for me without asking me if I wanted Him to do that for me! I was angry because His dying for me left me without control over my own life, for I could not reject someone who had done so much for me. My feelings were ones of being forced by Jesus' Love into being a Christian, giving my life to Him, and not being able to spend my life in the way in which I had planned. No wonder I could not talk with Jesus face-to-face in my prayer—a part of me was deeply angry with Him!

I quickly found my retreat master and explained to him what I had discovered. He asked me if I knew the meaning of these feelings and I assured him that I did. In confessing them aloud in the presence of my crucified Lord, He and I were reconciled. I could accept His Love for me more fully than ever before. This is another way to understand the veil that I sensed between Jesus and me in prayer; for in prayer Jesus was trying to love me, but at a deep level of my being I was rejecting that

Love, saying it was the reason that I could not live the life I had planned to live. I had chosen anger as the definition of myself and so I created a false self. The anger became a barrier, a veil between Jesus and me. But it was through the prayer of quiet that this situation was resolved and I was freed.

Now I am sure that Jesus wants to communicate with me and lead me personally on my path of spiritual growth. Not, as I said above, that this direct communication is a constant in my life, for both the Lord and I have reasons for drawing out of that direct communication now and then. But, in general, Jesus wants me to know His will so that I can do His will. The growing confidence within me that Jesus will reveal all that I need to know (Eph 1:9–10) makes it easier for me to listen, easier for me to obey as the months and years go by. Still, being able to hear God's voice is something that comes only with dedication, with a willingness to admit my mistakes, and with a deep love for Jesus and all He wants to do.

A Sample Prayer

It is not possible to write a true sample prayer in this case, for the prayer of quiet is just what is says. This sample prayer, then, will instead be a prayer preparing us for and opening us to using the prayer of quiet in our lives.

Before we begin this prayer, let us turn back for a moment to the very last section of the Preface and review the four steps that will help us prepare to pray. They are in the section entitled "A Note on Using the Sample Prayers in This Book." Once we have taken the time to complete these simple preparations we can begin to pray.

"Dear Jesus, thank You for living within me. Thank You for that presence within which is my strength, my hope, and my peace. Thank You that You love me, especially in all those areas that are sinful and therefore need Your loving the most.

"Jesus, I need to know my true self. I need to grow

spiritually and discover who I am in Your sight. I need to be able to hear You directly and completely. I know, Lord, that when I will hear You in that way, my life will be powerful—it will have direction, meaning, value—for Your wisdom will then be able to guide my every step. When I look at life from this point of view, my entire being longs for that time in which You will be completely alive within me.

"But, Lord, in order to get from this point to that, I need some special help. My life now is not as powerful as it could be and it is not directed by You because I cannot hear Your voice within me as well as I need to hear it. I want to hear Your voice, Jesus, but I am afraid—afraid of all the energy I will need to expend to get to that place in life, afraid of the secrets in my heart that I yet need to face, afraid of the times of frustration and discouragement that I know will face me if I choose to walk down this road that leads to a deeper relationship with You.

"Jesus, Your beloved apostle taught us that Your perfect Love casts out all fear. I need to know Your Love for me now so that I can start down this road. I need to be completely assured that when I choose not to be diligent in my search for You You will not reject me. I need to know that You are hoping with me and for me, and not betting against me (as I often do, and so expect others to do as well). Jesus, let us now spend some time together so that I can feel Your Love surrounding me and melting my fear. . . .

"Jesus, I will need perseverance to pray the prayer of quiet. I now consciously and deliberately ask for the grace of perseverance. I declare my intention to You that I want to stand against all the confusing forces within me—all the voices that have been fighting for attention ever since they were disordered by sin. I want order in my inner self so that I can hear You and then do whatever You ask of me. For I know, Jesus, that when I am able to do Your will more perfectly, I

will achieve the fulfillment of all the deepest desires of my heart. For You have baptized me into a nature that yearns to do Your will and to grow spiritually, and I will not be happy until I allow that nature to fulfill its purpose and goal.

"Thank You, Jesus, for hearing my prayer. Show me the way, Lord, and I will follow. I love You, Jesus. Show me how we can free that love completely so that we can be closer and more intimate friends. Amen."

Study Guide

1. Describe a time in which, and the process by which, you became aware of God's will in your life.
2. Which inner voices do you hear most frequently? Which are most distracting? Which are most helpful? How do you allow them to control your life?
3. How have you been taught to believe that Christ lives within you and guides you?
4. Describe a time in which you were praying to hear guidance and were mistaken in what you heard. What were the effects of following that "guidance"?
5. How will you rearrange your day to find a time for the prayer of quiet, or how will you rearrange your prayer time to include this prayer?

Suggested Reading

Bednarski, Sister Gloriana, RSM. *Listening for the Lord.* West Mystic, CN: Twenty-Third Publications, 1977.

Kelsey, Morton T. *The Other Side of Silence.* New York: Paulist Press, 1976.

Lewis, C. S. *Perelandra.* New York: Macmillan, 1965.

Chapter 3
Journal-Keeping

There are several fine books and some excellent courses available today that explain how to keep a journal, the benefits of doing so, and the theory of how journal-keeping helps us find our true selves and grow spiritually. Obviously, in the pages we will give to this subject we cannot cover all of this material, even in summary fashion, nor would we want to do so.

This chapter, then, will investigate the relationship between inner healing and journal-keeping. We will view journal-keeping as a form of written prayer, a valuable means of spiritual growth through inner healing and bringing forth the true self. We wish to affirm all who are already keeping a journal while possibly showing them new ways to use it, especially for inner healing; and we also wish to encourage others who have never kept a journal, and those who have given up the practice, to experiment with it as a means of growth in relationship to Jesus.

General Principles

Our modern world has a shallow view of who human beings are, and because each of us lives in this world, we are affected by it and its systems of thought. The society in which we live seems to tell us that our identity can be found in the work we produce, the things we own, the pleasure we experience, and the sexual fulfillment we find. Thus our society can easily dismiss the human rights of those chronically out of work, of the imprisoned, and of others—for example, unborn children, whom our society finds it convenient to abort and destroy, even though Jesus greatly loved those who were poor, sick, and otherwise powerless. Also, we cannot imagine ourselves living an economically simple life-style, even if that is what the Gospel teaches, but rather we become consumed with consuming. Further, we find suffering to be the most abhorrent experience of all, and we are often unwilling to endure it even when it is the kind of suffering that will enforce a value or bring spiritual growth—that is, suffering for the sake of the Gospel. When we deny ourselves the sexual pleasure that our society encourages, our society further makes it difficult for us to believe that we can still be adequate human beings, even though Jesus teaches us that our adequacy is based on our spiritual adoption by God.

This shallow view of the meaning of human life produces much illness, confusion, and emotional/spiritual disorientation (a kind of sickness of the inner self) in the people who believe it, and those people seem to constitute a majority of our society. When we believe that the goal of life is work, money, and pleasure, we ignore our all-too-real but hidden spiritual needs. They are hidden because they are not material and we cannot see them, and in a world that is prejudiced by materialism, we tend not to treat as real anything that we cannot know by apprehension through our physical bodies.

If we ignore any real bodily needs we will become physically ill. By not paying attention to our inner life we will become emotionally confused, form unsuccessful relationships, and never reach our full potential as human beings. The facts that link both physical illness and emotional disorientation to a lack of sound spirituality are surprising to many, yet they are formidable.

For example, the number-one killing disease in our society today is heart disease. Medical research is showing that, in many cases, those who have this disease also have a compulsive need to work and produce. They also tend to eat the wrong foods, do little exercise, and use stimulants like caffeine and depressants like nicotine. A sound spirituality confronts a person on each of these points and makes that person deal with them. Having heart disease, then, cannot infrequently be interpreted as a bodily signal to a person to understand with greater depth the meaning and purpose of life (a religious issue) and to upgrade the quality of life (a goal that can best be accomplished with a balanced spiritual, emotional, intellectual, and physical program).

The second major killer in our society is cancer. The causes of cancer are unknown, but many doctors are finding that the disease bears a high statistical correlation to emotional factors like stress, anxiety, and grief. Some doctors are suggesting that if we cannot handle these emotional situations in a healthy and creative way, cancer can be one physical expression of this emotional energy. Some even believe that upward of 70 percent of all cancer cases are psychosomatic (meaning that the body and the psyche interacting bring about the disease). This means that many of these cases could be prevented—and possibly even cured—by applying sound spiritual principles that lead to a healthy body, mind, and spirit. This premise is discussed at length in Dennis and Matthew Linn's *Healing Life's Hurts* (Paulist Press, 1978).

The third killing disease is circulatory problems; these are problems related to heart disease, which we have already discussed. The fourth killer is accidents. While on the surface there would seem to be no possibility for psychological or spiritual causes here, researchers have discovered that over 80 percent of all accidents in our country happen to 10 percent of the people, a fact that leads some to conclude that there is such a thing as an accident-prone personality and to posit a hypothesis that many accidents are psychogenic (i.e., they find their origins in the psyche). Therefore, it seems that sound spiritual principles applied to the lives of accident-prone people may be able to assist them in reducing the danger in their lives due to accidents.

The fifth killing disease in our society is cirrhosis, a disease of the liver often caused by ingestion of alcohol to excess; it is therefore a common disease in alcoholics. Alcoholism touches one out of five people in Western society, and it originates in deep tragedies of the soul. The sixth killer is suicide, and it is obvious that this is an emotional and spiritual problem at its roots.

In other words, the facts show that while we are materially more fulfilled than any other society that has ever appeared on the face of the earth, the quality of our living is quite low indeed. Statistics show that depression finds its way into the lives of one out of six people, alcoholism into one out of five, and cancer into one out of four. Many doctors and psychologists suggest that the major problem in our society today is loneliness, and that this is the deeper cause of much antisocial behavior, for example, crime. We are a society that claims to enjoy life, but, as the facts show, we do not know how to live healthy lives and we do not know who we are.

Jesus has a path for us to follow, a journey for us to take, so that we can be healthy in our bodies and in our inner selves, so that we can grow spiritually.

"And now the life you have [i.e., your true self, your identity] is hidden with Christ in God" (Col 3:3). The journey to health and identity is a journey to God, a spiritual journey. We can look for life in as many places as our society has. We can look for it in work, prestige, money, pleasure, sexual fulfillment, ease, power, even in human relationships, but we will never completely find it in these places. For our lives are hidden, they are hidden in Christ, and "when Christ is revealed—and he is your life—you too will be revealed in all your glory with him" (Col 3:4). In other words, we will find the fullness of life only when we find the fullness of Christ. That discovery begins now, but it will reach its uttermost completeness in the apocalyptic Day of the Lord.

What does all this have to do with journal-keeping? Simply, a journal is the way of uncovering our true selves hidden with Christ. It is like a gyroscope that helps us to keep our bearings as we travel our journey to the Father. It is a way of coming to know the Christ within, in Whom our true selves are kept for safekeeping. It is also, then, a way to raise the spiritual quality of our living. It is a way to grow spiritually.

We may wonder, if a journal is so important to the Christian life, how people in previous centuries lived Christian lives without journal-keeping, as it seems that many did. The answer is simple, if we are aware of the difference between our culture and others that have preceded it.

It was not until the period of the French Enlightenment that Western civilization began to develop an entirely secular view of the world. Before that time a religious world view was common. Practically everyone believed in God, received a tradition of Christian or at least religious morals, and in some sense understood the reality of the spiritual world. As a matter of course, people found a deep meaning for their inner lives in religion, religious experience, and religious rituals. It was not uncommon for a writer, composer, or head of state to adopt a religious principle as the basis for his or her work. It was not unusual for people to talk publicly about their religious beliefs and experiences. In other words, the culture supported individuals in a religious world view in which they could discover their identity and find health, wholeness, and meaning for their lives.

Today, if anything, the opposite is true. Our society not only is unsupportive of a religious view of the world, but it often denigrates people who have such a view. Religious convictions are not the commonly held assumptions that they were in other cultures, and belief is considered to be a personal affair. Therefore, our society and many of the forces within it do not give Christians the support we need to continue growing in our identities, in our health and wholeness, and in a sense of the meaning and value of our lives. What society chooses not to do, Christian community and the personal journal must replace; otherwise, we will lose our bearings and fall victim to one or several of the destructive pressures in society mentioned above.

A Description of the Prayer

What is a journal and how does it work? A journal is a record of insights, prayers, spiritual intuitions, significant events, dreams, and reflections—all products of our inner selves. When we write a journal we ask ourselves, "What are the significant thoughts and feelings of this day? What are my

responses to them? Did they come from any particular events?"
And then we write our answers. A journal, then, is a material or
physical sign of the movements of our minds and spirits, of the
movements of Jesus within us, of the result of God's grace in
our lives. Considered in this way, journals are, in the words of
Morton Kelsey, our personal sacraments.

A journal works partially through the psychological meaning we give to writing. When we write something, we are
telling ourselves that it is important. Because writing takes time
and energy, we do not waste it on things that have little value to
us. And as our culture develops into one of telecommunications,
the act of writing takes on greater significance.

Similarly, when we write an inner experience, we are telling ourselves that our inner experiences are important. In a
world that tells us that only material things and their effects are
important, keeping a journal teaches us the true value of our
own inner selves; for, if we follow completely the values of the
world, we will conclude that our inner selves have no value and
only material things have value. The materialism of our society
keeps us from discovering our true selves, simply by telling us
that our inner selves are unreal, mechanistic, or unimportant.
Journal-keeping is one of a few activities that help us find our
true identity and that directly contradict the shallow view of
mankind prevalent in society today.

A journal also works because it is a way of remembering.
Many of our religious experiences will be lost to us unless we
have a way of remembering them. Because our lives are filled
with details, because our lives are busy, we need a place to keep
and treasure those moments in which we have touched our true
selves and in which the Lord has touched us. If some important
dignitary of the world visited us in our homes, we would look
for keepsakes by which to remember that event—pictures, mem-
orabilia, perhaps a newspaper article describing the event. But
when Jesus comes to visit us, we do not treat His visits with the
same importance: We have no keepsakes—unless we learn to
keep a journal and ourselves record what happened.

Again, a journal works because it preserves the concrete-
ness of our religious experiences. An hour after we have a

profound experience with the Lord we can easily wonder whether it was real. With a little emotional distance, we can say that it was all a "figment of our imaginations" (although the phrase itself is a sad commentary on the way our culture views imagination) even though when it was actually happening it was as real as anything we have ever experienced. One reason this may happen so easily is the prejudice in our culture against treating inner events as real. Even though our minds intellectually accept the idea that our spirits can know spiritual realities just as our bodies can know physical realities, our final acceptance of religious experience is influenced by the assumption in our culture that spiritual things are not real, and therefore are not valuable.

Similarly, if we have a vague religious experience (in other words, an experience in which we cannot know with much detail what has happened) or if we cannot discover our reactions to our experience, the experience will become clear and concrete to us as we write it—difficult an endeavor as that sometimes is. Words help to make things definite. As long as we merely think about our experience, we run the risk of not seeing its importance. But when we think by writing, it is more probable that the experience will make sense to us and that we will find its value in our lives. As E. M. Forster once said, "How can I know what I think until I see what I say?"

Keeping a journal, then, means taking fifteen to thirty minutes several days a week to record important things we have thought, felt, dreamed, prayed, or experienced in relationships. One day we may wish to pray by writing a letter to Jesus, which we record in our journals. Another day we may write out our dreams of the night before and then ask the Lord to help us interpret them. On another occasion we may want to write out our reflections on a particular relationship and its importance in our lives. In other words, it does not have to be a complicated endeavor; it can be quite simple. All that is important is that we are honest and try to look beyond our surface feelings and reactions when we write. This requirement is both simple and difficult.

Honesty is difficult because we often do not find it pleasant to face ourselves, especially our deepest weaknesses and strengths. We do not like to face our weaknesses because they make us feel inadequate and insecure (until we face them); we do not like to face our strengths because then we must take responsibility for using them, and we lose our excuses for saying we cannot change.

Therefore, in beginning a journal, people often feel as if someone is looking over their shoulder, making it difficult for them to be honest; then they begin to write their journal for someone else to read, revealing only the things they would want other people to know. Usually this reaction is a projection of an inner struggle: "Shall I let my right hand know what my left hand is doing?" Another way this struggle manifests itself is the subtle temptation to write "for posterity." This is the feeling that says we should not put down on paper anything we would not want to leave behind us, anything by which we would not want to be remembered. Both of these reactions are signs that the true self wants to come forth, and it is being halted by the false self—that self which is due to sin and hurt. Honesty in journal-keeping allows us to find our true selves.

Finding our deepest feelings can also be difficult. We often find it convenient to hide behind certain socially acceptable reactions to life, not admitting that our own deep and personal reactions may be highly unacceptable or unconventional. Again, these deeper reactions often make us feel inadequate and insecure until we face them. But if we are to find the vitality and the joy of discovering who we really are (and the Christ in Whom our true selves are hidden), if we are to know that we are not like everyone else but are unique, created so by God, and found beautiful in our uniqueness by Him, we need to look well at the person He created, not at the person we want to be, think we ought to be, or think others expect us to be.

Also, we do not like to search for our deepest feelings because then we must admit that we do not know who we really are, and admitting that makes us feel foolish, confused, or without control over our lives. But who told us that it is *wrong* to feel foolish, confused, or out of control? Surely not God, before Whom and in comparison to Whom no one is wise and powerful. We must be careful concerning to whom we listen and what we believe!

So we learn to move beyond prayers like "Please bless so-and-so" and "Thank You for the wonderful things in my life" in our journals unless they truly are our deepest feelings on that particular day. When we do so, we will be moving aside the less important elements of our lives to make room for our true selves to come forth. This is a beginning of spiritual growth.

An Example

Several years ago, a woman came to me extremely distressed and confused. She was physically beautiful, with a tall, model-like figure, but she saw herself as ugly. She was in her late twenties but looked ten years older from worry and fear. She would awaken in the middle of the night shaking violently and perspiring, and during the day she could not concentrate long enough, for example, even to decide what breakfast cereal to feed her children.

While I was not qualified to make a psychological diagnosis, it seemed to me that she was close to a nervous breakdown. This I surmised when she looked at me with little-girl eyes and said: "I don't know what I am going to do. I don't think I can make it. Do you think I will make it?" She repeated this question several times.

We talked about many things in our weekly sessions together. She asked me to assure her each week that she would find her way out of this confusion (I was relying on God's power to heal, not on my abilities as a counselor nor on her strength of personality, when I assured her she would). We prayed prayers for healing of memories (described in Part Two), and asked Jesus to help her find her true self. She had lost touch with her true self by succumbing to many pressures in her life—no one of which would have had the power to break her, but which as a totality indeed did have that power.

She was not able to communicate with her husband and felt totally unsupported and unloved. She was under constant pressure from her mother-in-law, who lived nearby. She felt out of place in her small town since she was of a different national extraction from everyone else there, including her husband's family. She had left the church of her childhood for her husband's when she married him, only to feel condemned by this church's teachings. And when her husband more or less demanded that she actively participate in this church's weekly activities, she felt no community support for the religious ideas that were most dear to her heart. Finally, she was raising all her children alone while also functioning as secretary for her husband's business—without a salary. She had lost her identity by living almost entirely by other people's values, needs, and demands in family and in church, and she no longer knew who she was.

So, after the initial visit, I began to teach her about her true self and how to discover it. We talked about finding time for herself just to relax or to do the things she wanted to do; we talked about the possibility of rejoining the church of her childhood; we talked about how to deal with the pressures of in-laws and demanding church structures (i.e., about how to say no); and we talked about keeping a journal.

While each of these elements helped her, she reported to me after she was well and functioning creatively again that the journal was most helpful. It was there that she learned how to be herself and how to accept herself, even and especially when no one else would. It was there that she found her deepest reactions to life—we must *find* our reactions before we can act on them—and it was there she discovered she had the courage in Jesus to live by the values that she and He thought best for her. It was there that she began to unravel for herself the confusing tangle of feelings and relationships that was her life.

While our sessions together were important and, especially at the beginning, even indispensable for support and encouragement, guidance, and a prayer partner, it was in her journal that she began to discover that she, on her own, could find and live a life that was creative and fulfilling. In that freedom she was able to rededicate herself in real love to those to whom she had committed her life—her husband, children, and church—while also setting limits on demands she would allow on herself and finding time to enjoy herself. She was able to affirm herself in Jesus and to see her beauty in Him.

What is she doing now? Many things she was not doing before. For example, both she and her husband have secretaries, and she counsels and prays with people herself. She has a renewed and loving relationship with her husband; her mother-in-law has become her best friend; and, in accepting the fact that her husband's church is different from the church of her youth, she has accepted the giftedness of their view of life without thinking she has to become like them or a part of them. Because she has learned to love herself as Jesus loves her, she is not only healed but is also a healing person for others.

A Sample Prayer

As was the case in the last chapter, it is not possible to write a sample prayer here, since a journal is an entirely personal prayer form. This prayer, then, will be one asking God to open us to keeping a journal, to keeping it in honesty, to finding our deepest feelings, and to give us a desire to know our true selves no matter what the personal cost, so that we can encourage our own spiritual growth.

As we begin this prayer, we need again to prepare. Let us turn back for a moment to the last section of the Preface and review the four steps that ready us for contacting the Lord. They are in the section entitled "A Note on Using the Sample Prayers in This Book."

> *"Lord Jesus, I come before You thankful that You have created me unique and beautiful in Your eyes. I thank You that You can see the 'real me,' even though I cannot always do so, even though I try to hide behind masks of social acceptability, conventionality, and an imitation of real Christian love. Jesus, I know that it is the real me whom You love, for that person You created. I, on the other hand, have created and allowed*

others to create a false self whom I have allowed to prevail while my true self has been submerged.

"Jesus, I need Your help. I need You to show me my true self. I need to see what You see in me. I need to feel Your Love if I am to grow spiritually, and it is only my true self that can feel Your Love.

"Jesus, show me Your will in the matter of my keeping a journal. Help me to be open to the possibilities of this tool in my life. Stir Your Spirit within me to help me understand with my heart, not only my mind, what a journal will do for me and for my relationship with You. I want You more than anything, Jesus, and if that means that I need to keep a journal, I am willing to do that.

"If a journal will help me to find my true self, Lord, I will need to be honest in it. That kind of honesty is a grace that only You can give, and I ask for it now. I want to be able to see myself with the Love with which You see me. To do that I need Your honesty—to see my strengths and weaknesses, to see my life, to take responsibility for being who I am, so that in Your Truth I can become free. If I look at myself in the context of Your Love, Jesus, I know I cannot feel depressed or conceited, inadequate or powerful, but I will rest in the security of Your caring, so deep and rich. And in that security, I will find my true self.

"I also need to know what my reactions to life are. So often I respond with someone else's thoughts and feelings. Stir Your Spirit within me to uncover these reactions, especially the ones I find unacceptable or fearsome. I need to face them sometime, and I want You to be with me when I do. Help me become aware of the many ways they reveal themselves in my thoughts, intuitions, moods, dreams, and relationships. Help me to learn how to write them, and I ask for the grace to persist in my writing even when it seems that all these reactions are blocked and not one of them will come through. Help me then to believe that You are *still with me and guiding this journey of spiritual growth to my true self and to Your Father.*

"Lord, last of all, I pray for a thirst—a thirst to know who I really am, a thirst that will not be satisfied by anything but that discovery. I ask You to make me uncomfortable until I set out on this journey, and I ask for a vision of my goal to spur me on. I ask You to love me in this way, so that I will find my true self and thus know what it means to be a child of God. Lord, I know that for everything valuable in life I must pay a price: I am willing to pay it no matter what it may be if it means that I will find You. For I love You, Jesus, and I know that You are the only real joy in life.

"Thank You, Jesus, for hearing my prayer and for teaching my heart what my mind cannot understand. I will follow You on this journey inward. Lead me, Lord, lead me. Amen."

Study Guide

1. Describe a time in your life in which you ignored one of your spiritual needs and explain the effects of doing so on your life.

2. What indications can you see, other than those presented in this book, that Western civilization has a narrow or limited view of who human beings are?

3. What are the signs in your life that you do not know how to live a healthy life? What alternatives for change lie before you?

4. With what arguments would you agree or disagree with the statement in this chapter that "the journey to health and identity is a journey to God, a spiritual journey"?

5. How does our society's secular view of the world affect your spiritual growth and the way you live? How does it affect the way you see yourself?

6. If you already keep a journal, explain some of the thoughts and feelings you have about its importance in your life; if you

do not now keep a journal, explain what you imagine your reaction would be to doing so.

7. Describe the relationship you see between honesty and mental health, and between honesty and spiritual growth.

Suggested Reading

Kelsey, Morton T. *The Other Side of Silence.* New York: Paulist Press, 1976.

Progoff, Ira. *At a Journal Workshop.* New York: Dialogue House Library, 1975.

Simons, George F. *Keeping Your Personal Journal.* New York: Paulist Press, 1976.

Chapter 4
Integrating and Balancing Opposites

There are many different ways to conceptualize personality. One of them is that the personality is a composite of opposites, opposing energies that balance each other in what psychologists call "homeostasis." According to this view, personality problems and disorders can originate or produce an imbalance within this delicate structure, and so restoring the balance is the goal of healing.

In my work with people I have found this conceptualization to be a valuable one, and I have learned to pray to integrate and balance opposites within the personality. Especially when I view this prayer as a part of a larger picture of religious therapy, combining it with other avenues toward spiritual growth and inner healing, I have found it to be a liberating element in people's lives.

For many of us, it is not difficult to see large areas in our lives that are out of balance: work and family, time for self and time for others, inner life and responsibilities to others, play and work. God does not call us to lead fragmented lives but integrated ones in which our values correspond to the needs of our true selves. And so He calls us to pray for balance within our personalities and to learn how to use the grace that comes from that prayer.

This chapter, then, will help us to do just that. In it we will attempt to find a more definite and concrete understanding of the many forces within our personalities and to learn how to help them grow under Jesus' direction and come to wholeness, that is, to find the power through the Holy Spirit for our hidden selves to grow strong (Eph 3:17).

General Principles

Our exterior lives often reflect our interior lives. When a person's living quarters are disheveled, there is usually some disorganization in his or her inner life; when one's relationships are in a constant state of brokenness, there is usually much brokenness and pain within that person's psyche and spirit as well. And so we know that when there are large areas of our lives out of balance, we can look to a partial disintegration within ourselves as a possible source of the problem.

Within our personalities are opposing energies almost too many to enumerate. Some of them are: intellect and emotion, masculine characteristics and feminine characteristics, needs to please others and needs to please ourselves, physical needs and spiritual needs, needs to work and needs to relax, seeing the way things are and seeing what we want them to be, hatred and love, hope and despair, faith and indifference, the parts of ourselves we reject and our conscious self-concept; the list could go on and on.

When problems arise in our lives—relationship problems, spiritual problems, psychological problems—they could easily involve one or more of these opposites being out of balance. Sometimes we need to discover why they are out of balance so that we can pray about the source of the problem as well; and sometimes all we need to do is to admit that there is a lack of balance in our lives and pray for it to be set aright. We need to pray that the poles of these opposites be integrated into each other; spiritual growth often results.

Unfortunately, this is not as easy as it sounds. For to admit some imbalance about our inner selves is not just to say that it is there, it is also to recognize that it needs to be changed, that the change will cause pain, and that we are willing to endure that pain for the sake of growth.

Also, to admit that there is a lack of integration and balance in our lives means we admit that we have made mistakes in judgment for which we need to forgive ourselves (Chapter 5), and because of pride and/or insecurity it is difficult for many of us to admit when we are wrong and need to change. Some also find it extremely difficult to ask sincerely for forgiveness.

Further, to admit there is a lack of integration and balance in our lives means to admit that we have harmed our lives in some way and we need to be saved from self-destruction. Again it is our pride and insecurity that prevent us from sincerely asking Jesus to help us.

But any of us who have tried it know that we cannot change much of our inner selves on our own. We can change a little part here, move a little bit there; but within a short period of time we find ourselves back where we started, behaving in the same way in which we used to behave. No matter how hard we work at it, by ourselves we cannot integrate any parts of our personalities, for they are connected to drives so deep within us that we often are unaware of them, and we definitely cannot control them. Our problem is that in some ways they are in control of us!

Only Christ can touch these deeper parts of ourselves and free us. Only He knows what is the proper balance for the different parts of our personalities so that we can express our true selves. We may have an idea of how we would like to be; but often if that idea were actually to come into being, we would be just as unhappy because of other problems that change would cause.

So admitting that there is a lack of balance in our lives means allowing Jesus to be God for us, allowing Him to be Lord, Savior, and Redeemer in our lives. It means admitting that because He is God and He made us, He knows better than we do how our lives need to be reshaped to become integrated, balanced, and successful—in His eyes.

Praying for integration within our personalities is something that needs to be done over and over again until we see the results we need. We often resist changes in the areas about which we are praying, because the changes for which we pray will demand that we act, think, and feel in new and often uncomfortable ways. Therefore, we both want and resist change, and are thus not entirely open to our own prayer. While this "approach/avoidance conflict" is a natural phenomenon, we need to recognize how important and powerful it is. It can keep us from receiving fully the grace of God. However, the grace that we are open to receive does come into us and works on our resistance little by little until the resistance weakens, crumbles, and disappears. But that process usually is the result of many, many prayers as well as other efforts aimed at our spiritual growth.

So we need to learn patience and aim for long term growth. What we are praying for in this kind of prayer is deep psychological and spiritual healing, a major reintegration of our personality structure that will have profound effects in our lives for years to come, and that will result in greater freedom for our true selves. These changes will affect the way we view life and its opportunities, our goals and dreams, our relationships, work and leisure. Especially because of the long-range effects of this kind of prayer, it is all the more advisable to allow Jesus to decide in which particular ways to integrate our personalities. In so doing, He will become the Lord of our inner lives and we will know the truth that Paul taught: "I have been crucified with Christ and I live now not with my own life but with the life of Christ who lives in me" (Gal 2:20).

A Description of the Prayer

Most of the times in which I pray this prayer I do so in the context of a larger prayer for inner healing; however, it can be prayed on its own. I find it comfortable to use the image of the Light of God, for light is energy. Physiologists tell us that our bodies run on a low current of electricity flowing through the nerves and brain cells; and this electric current "carves impressions" on the cortex of the brain as we repeat thoughts, feelings, and actions. As these impressions become deeper we form a habit of that particular reaction. The imbalance in ourselves that we perceive is in part "pressed into" our brains by the electricity in our bodies; and so I find it helpful to pray that these impressions are washed over by the Light of God's Love, that this Light erases old and unhealthy patterns of thought, feeling, and behavior and creates new, healthier, more balanced ones.

But our patterns of thought, feeling, and behavior are not only in our brains, for our brains are the material tools of our psyches. This part of us also needs the Light of God. If there is physical imbalance in our brains, we know the deeper psychic energies within are also out of balance, and so we ask that Light flow into our psyches, strengthening energies that ought not be so weak, slowing energies that ought not be so strong.

First of all, we need integration among the four major parts of the psyche: intellect, will, imagination, and memory. Quite often in life we develop one or two of these functions more strongly than the others, and in so doing place our psyches, and therefore our lives, in a state of imbalance. It is especially common among some people that intellect and will are developed while imagination and memory are largely ignored; this can happen when we do not dedicate these functions to God (Chapter 1). Others live in a world dominated by memories or phantasy images to the exclusion of logic, new ideas, and efforts of the will. God never meant that one of these functions should completely dominate our inner lives, for each has a unique gift to bring into our lives. Therefore, we need to admit we need integration among these functions of our minds.

And within each of these functions, the contents of our intellects, wills, imaginations, and memories need to be in balance—that is, the various thoughts, values, and feelings by which our lives operate. When one of these begins to dominate us, we become as beings possessed; we cannot see the total reality of life for the one goal we have. A healthy life means a more balanced existence, and the Lord wants us to pray that the Light of His Love influence our psyches and their contents with insight into the purpose of our entire lives.

On a physiological level, another form of imbalance we can experience is an imbalance of hormones and other secretions within the body (often subtly connected with movements of the psyche), and imbalances within and among various organs of the body. Often it is not certain whether these reactions are causes or effects of imbalances within the psyche, but we do know that they affect the way in which we live and relate to other people. So we can find it worthwhile to pray that the Light of God will fill any parts of our bodies not acting in harmony with the rest of the body, and that the Light of God will balance all hormonal and other secretions in the body in the best way for us. We do not need to have all the particular medical knowledge of what is wrong to ask God to set it right, although that knowledge can help our prayers to be more specific.

Finally, we pray for a balance between ourselves and the world. We can pray that our interior responsibilities and exterior responsibilities do not overwhelm each other, if they have been doing so in the past. We can pray for balance in relationships—between psychological dependence and independence, between two personalities one of which is strong and the other weak, between needs for community and needs for privacy, between needs to work and needs to relax. We ask that the Light of God illumine any areas that may confine us, and that He strengthen any part of us that needs to express itself more fully in the context of the Life of Jesus.

If we have begun our prayer asking the Lord to send His Light into our inner selves to bring forth all that needs to be known and faced, then we need also to pray for the grace to submit to whatever is necessary in the Lord's eyes to accomplish the healing we are requesting. In other words, we conclude with a prayer that we have no resistance to Him and what He wants to do in our lives. What would be the sense of asking Him to do something if, when He did it, we would only resist it? Rather, we want our attitude to be one of cooperation, even though we do not know what He will want to do. Our trust in Him will determine how decisively and quickly He will be able to act and help us with our problems.

An Example

A married couple came to me with a deep hurt between them; since they could no longer talk with each other, they needed to talk with a third party. After being with both of them for a while it was obvious to me that this was a case in which both the husband and wife had believed the American stereotype of what it means to be male and female: he was detached emotionally, overly logical in his opinions, and confused by displays of feelings and by needs for creativity; she, on the other hand, was given to outbursts of various emotions, had not developed her rational mind to any great extent, and was in touch with her feelings and expressed with great intensity that she was hurt, angry, and miserable in this relationship.

Since the marriage was more than ten years old, it took quite some time for them to see that in a sense, unconsciously, they had planned things this way, that each had chosen the role he or she played because at one time it had been comfortable for him or her and for the other as well. For early in the marriage he did not want to threaten his macho image by admitting that he was sensitive and had deep feelings, and she did not want to threaten her femininity by being strong and assertive. So they had made an unconscious contract to behave in the way in which they indeed were now behaving.

But after several years, the convenience of this arrangement began to erode. While at first she had wanted her man to be strong, rational, and independent, she was now feeling a need for him to be sensitive to her feelings and to give her understanding; and while he originally enjoyed his wife when she could express her feelings and his own as well, and he thought her comical when she could not follow his ideas, now he was needing her to look at life from his point of view once in a while and to be able to act more independently in making her own decisions.

Also, they began to dislike themselves the way they were, and they began to blame each other for it. She could not see her own worth and value because he would never affirm it, for he was now looking for things she could not and/or would not give him; he was almost constantly angry at everyone—which revealed a deep anger toward himself—because he did not sense that he was important, nor were his opinions valuable, to his wife.

Once we unraveled this complicated tangle of ideas, expectations, and emotions, the couple saw that each needed to find more balance in his or her life so that their relationship could express the mutuality they were seeking. Each saw the internal lack of balance in both of them as the cause of their relationship problems, and they were motivated to grow as well as to go through the painful process of allowing their relationship to change, that is, to change the ways they needed each other, their expectations of each other, their individual participation in their family life, and their needs for time outside the family.

While none of this was easy or simple, the beacon of hope we all had through this process was the prayer for integration and balance. At first we prayed that Jesus would bring about in both of them a new integration within their own personalities, that under the Spirit's guidance they would discover and act on new capabilities within themselves—that he would discover his ability to be sensitive and she her ability to be assertive. Then we prayed that between them God would establish an order with the grace of understanding and patience. In praying for a balance in their relationship we asked the Lord to help them discover and cherish in themselves the parts of themselves that were like the other. The rest of our prayers included forgiveness (Chapter 5) for past hurts and healing of memories (Part Three) for experience of their marriage, both individually and as a couple. But the majority of our praying centered on discovering their true selves by praying for integration of opposites within their personalities.

This was the beginning of great change and growth in them as persons and as a couple. After an initial four weekly visits, I saw them individually or as a couple once every two or three months for approximately three years. Over that period of time she began to organize her time better and to find new ways to express herself, including working for a while. He found himself growing in his ability to listen to her feelings and to understand her hurt. They decided to attend a Marriage Encounter weekend and their communication benefited greatly from that experience—and that was something both of them would have resisted before praying to discover their true selves.

Their marriage and family problems smoothed out with counseling and prayer, and with much work and time. Part of the hard work involved was the difficulty they experienced in allowing the Lord to help them grow, but especially in accepting the ways their spouse was growing. It was a time of "creative instability" in their marriage, when they did not know definitely what to expect from themselves, let alone from each other; but in that freedom the Lord had a chance to work and show them how to love each other in the ways they needed to be loved.

A Sample Prayer

Before we begin to pray this prayer, let us review the four steps that will help us to pray, listed in the Preface under the section entitled "A Note on Using the Sample Prayers in This Book." When we have completed these simple instructions we can begin to pray.

"Lord Jesus, this is an area of deep healing within me, and I'm not sure I understand all about it nor that I ever could. All I really know is that no one can grow through life perfectly integrated and balanced, and so I need You in my personality. I ask You to stir Your Spirit within me to show me why my life needs Your sense of balance, and to show me in what particular areas I need it. . . .

"Jesus, I know that there are certain areas of my life that are governed by habits of thought, feeling, and behavior that throw my life out of balance. I ask now that the Light of Your Love for me wash over my brain where all these habits are physically ingrained. I ask You to free me with Your grace and create in me new

*patterns of thought, feeling, and behavior more in tune
with the person I really am, and so free me to express
my true self. . . .*

"Lord, I need that same Light also in my psyche.
Integrate more fully my intellect, will, imagination,
and memory. Especially, Jesus, if one of these functions
is overdeveloped in me, bring it into balance with the
others. Also, please integrate more fully the ways my
body, psyche, and spirit function; under the guidance
of Your Light, let the energy of Your Love flow
through me and bring these three basic parts of me into
harmony with each other and with You. . . .

"If there is any thought, value, or feeling that has
dominated my life, Lord, I ask You to reveal it to me
now. . . .Show me how my life and my relationships
have been affected by this compulsive reaction. . . . Jesus, I invite Your healing Light into this reaction to
put it in its proper place in harmony with the rest of
my life. I sense Your Light coming into me now,
releasing the tension that this imbalance has wrought
and creating new possibilities for the way in which I
will react in the future.

"Lord Jesus, if in my body there is any imbalance
of hormonal or other secretions that is causing or is the
result of disorientations within my psyche, I ask You
now to heal that imbalance. Send the Light of Your
Love into those parts of my body that are not functioning according to Your perfect plan for me, and help my
body to accept Your Love, which will make it whole.
Jesus, only You know how fully this physical imbalance has affected my life; I give You permission to put
back into proper perspective all those parts of my life
touched by this problem. Thank You, Jesus, for knowing what to do and how to do it gently and effectively.

"And now, Lord, I ask You to balance all the great
tensions in my life, all the opposites within me. Help
me to take the time to accept your healing Light into
each of these areas of my life; my masculine character-

*istics and my feminine characteristics ... my intellect
and my emotions ... my body and spirit ... my personal needs and my responsibilities to others ... the personality traits within me that I like and those that I
don't like ... my self-concept as a sinner and my desire
to be godly ... my needs to please others and my needs
to please myself ... my loves and my hatreds ... my
hope and despair ... my faith and my indifference ...
the joy of my life and the sorrow.... Thank You, Lord,
that You heal them all, that You integrate them all in
just the way You see they need to be.*

*"Jesus, I know that all this integration will not
happen without many changes in my life, and these
changes will each bring its own kind of pain as well as
joy. So I ask You to stay with me always and be my
strength to bear the pain of change that leads to spiritual growth. Thank You, Jesus, for understanding the
delicacy of my inner self and for respecting it. Integrate my personality so that I will be free to express
my true self and so give You all the praise and glory
You have intended for my life. Amen."*

Study Guide

1. What areas in your life seem to be out of balance? What feelings does this state of affairs elicit within you?
2. Describe a situation in your life that you can see was caused by a loss or lack of integration within you.
3. Has pride or insecurity ever kept you from changing the way you live? Describe one situation in which pride or insecurity affected you in this way.
4. Describe a time in which prayer helped you to balance your life. Did coming into balance make you feel comfortable, uncomfortable, or both? Explain.
5. What are your feelings about the possibility that you will have to endure a time of "creative instability" as you pray for greater integration in areas of your life which may need it?

Suggested Reading

Baars, Conrad W., M.D. *Feeling and Healing Your Emotions.* Plainfield, N.J.: Logos International, 1979.

Sanford, Agnes. *The Healing Light,* Plainfield, N.J.: Logos International, 1978.

Sanford, John. *The Invisible Partners,* New York: Paulist Press, 1980.

Stapleton, Ruth Carter. *The Experience of Inner Healing.* Waco, TX: Word, Inc., 1978.

Part Two

Freeing the True Self

Introduction
We Submit to Christ's Truth and Follow Him

"If you make my word your home you will indeed be my disciples, you will learn the truth and the truth will make you free" (Jn 8:31–32).

The Spirit and the Psyche

Discovering our true selves is not enough. Knowing who we really are is a beginning; becoming free to use our true selves in service to the Kingdom of God is the next step. We need to find the freedom of the children of God (Rom 8:21).

This freedom begins by acknowledging the difference and complementarity between our minds and our spirits. For the freedom for which we search is a spiritual freedom, a freedom that will come from God and into us through our spirits. Our spiritual growth depends on our finding this kind of freedom.

Deeper than our psyches—that is, our intellects, wills, imaginations, and memories—are our spirits (Heb 4:12). Our spirits comprise the functions of communion (the ability, desire, and need each person has to worship God), conscience (the ability to know right from wrong), and spiritual intuition (our ability to receive the Gifts of the Holy Spirit).

Our spirits are the deepest part of us and, therefore, are the most important, for it is in our spirits that we contact the spiritual world—spiritual creatures and God. It is in our spirits, then, that we reach out for that without which nothing else has value or worth—life and freedom. We need to know the nature of our spirits so that we can enter the spiritual world and grow spiritually.

Yet many segments of modern culture and even some segments of the Church seem to have lost sight of what our spirits are and of how they interact with the rest of our human nature. Many centuries ago, when philosophy had its beginnings, one way human beings began to conceive human nature was as a union between body and soul. This dualistic notion is quite different from the biblical tripartite view of human nature as body, mind, and spirit. In the dualistic view the functions of the mind and the spirit are joined in the concept called "soul." However, as they are joined they are more easily confused, for they are not seen as distinct. Later certain segments of Christian theology began to be influenced by this philosophy and therefore began to lose a sense of the uniqueness of the spirit as different from the mind. Along with this loss came a lesser understanding of what the spirit does, how it works, and most important, how it is broken and how it is healed. This philosophical and theological problem is important to us because through the centuries these notions have entered our everyday thinking.

Thus, Western culture was ripe for the final blow. From the time of the Renaissance until the present, our culture has been fascinated with the powers and potentials of the human mind. This interest in the development of the mind in itself can be good; but because in our cultural thinking the distinction between mind and spirit was more or less vague, interest in the spirit, the spiritual world, and spiritual growth began to be submerged. One example of this situation is the way many people throughout the ages, but especially today, define *faith* as primarily an intellectual assent to truth and not also as a spiritual gift, a way of living in which a person is committed to Christ as his personal savior, and only after that as an assent to the truth He teaches.

Thus, in our age we have, to a great extent, lost contact

with the spiritual world in which each of us lives, whether or not we learn how to live in it well, and in doing so we have stunted our spiritual growth. We find our culture to be one of people who are often rootless, aimless, depressed, in identity crisis, and lonely—and, with all our intellectual knowledge and all our technological advances, we cannot seem to help them much. Our society invents program after program to solve these problems, and when they do not accomplish their goals we do not know the reason. As we look at our society from this point of view, we are able to state the reason generally in this way: These problems at their roots are really spiritual problems, calling for spiritual healing and spiritual growth. Yet very few people today understand the spiritual world or even their own spirits. Similarly, very few people have the skills needed to ask God to free their inner selves and to grow spiritually.

The Freedom Our Inner Selves Need

The first freedom that our inner selves need is the freedom of our spirits from our minds. In the Preface we learned that spirit and mind are separate, nonmaterial parts of our inner selves. However, when we are born into the world we do not experience these two parts of us as operating separately.

We do not experience our spirits as different from our minds because, when we come into this world controlled by sin, our spirits are deadened by that sin. Our bodies and minds are alive through physical birth; our spirits must be brought alive through spiritual rebirth. We are reborn when we accept the Word of God into our hearts and let Jesus become our Savior from the sin that has deadened our spirits. "The word of God is something alive and active: it cuts like any double-edged sword but more finely: it can slip through the place where the soul (or mind) is divided from the spirit" (Heb 4:12).

Until we experience the power of the Word of God to save our spirits from death, we do not experience our spirits or a spiritual life. We function as if our minds are the part of us that can produce our greatest achievements; the works of our intellect, wills, and imaginations—that is, philosophy, the sciences, good works, and the arts, in other words, humanism—become our goals. However, without our spirits to guide us, our humanistic efforts, while they may do much good along the way, will ultimately lead us to failure, for they cannot be filled with the goodness and holiness of God.

To live a full life we need to experience ourselves fully—as body, mind, *and spirit*. When we accept Jesus as our Savior, then, we are first beginning to live fully. This acceptance of Jesus is both something that is a gift from God (often celebrated in the rite of Baptism) and something we take into our hearts consciously (in an adult experience of conversion to Jesus) if it is to be fully effective in our lives. Therefore, while we may have been baptized as infants or even as adults, if we have not consciously made a choice to allow Jesus to be free in our spirits, and to allow His Spirit to be free in us, then we may find it difficult to experience spiritual growth on a day-to-day basis.

If this is the case for us, we can alter our situation right now, if we want to. First, let us pray for the grace of sincerity and for the desire to let Jesus and His Spirit be free within us. When we sense that desire growing within us, we pray:

> *"Jesus, thank You for saving me on the Cross. Thank You for Your Love, infinitely deep. Thank You that Your Love can enter my spirit and set me free to live a full life, experiencing every part of me. Jesus, today I acknowledge You not only as Savior of the world, but also as my own personal Savior. I ask You to come into my heart completely. I ask You to set my spirit free from Satan's influence and activity as I renounce him and all his works. I give You permission to take charge of the direction of my life, and to help me to experience my full heritage as Your friend and fellow family member, the Gifts of the Holy Spirit."*

This prayer, prayed sincerely, will begin to free our spirits from the domination of our minds. From this time on, we will begin to experience our spirits as different from our minds, leading us in different directions, giving us different goals, adding a richness and a depth to our lives, showing us the true value of the products of our minds. This is the first healing that our inner selves need. . . .

Another kind of freedom we need is revealed by one of the saddest trends in our society today, the breaking up of families, not only in divorce, although that is sad enough, but also in alienation, disaffection, cruelty, and violence. It seems quite clear that less and less do people know how to live with each other. Many people walk through their lives watching significant and important relationships disintegrate in crises as if there were nothing they could do about it. Death, illness, financial troubles, and the like bring pressure on people who then say and do things that hurt those around them. Yet we have forgotten how to forgive, how to let go of grievances, how to apologize, and even how to accept forgiveness from another.

Forgiveness is a cleansing and freeing power for our inner selves. It is the other side of the coin of love: Love forms relationships, and when they are broken, forgiveness is the glue that puts them back together again. Yet we have come to prize so much our own ideas, our own ways of doing things, our own attitudes about the way life should be, that when life brings us to a choice between these on the one hand and our relationships on the other, we often choose our own little world and its loneliness.

Jesus, on the other hand, always chose relationships, and therefore He spoke of forgiveness so frequently that we could easily say that He saw it as the first step into the Kingdom of God, the first step of spiritual growth. Without forgiveness— both receiving and giving it—our spirits remain dead, unregenerated, or broken. And when that is the state of our spirits, that will also be the state of our relationships with others. . . .

C. S. Lewis said that Satan's greatest trick is to convince people that he does not exist. Our modern Western civilization has been well fooled, according to Lewis's standards, and the results can be seen in our newspapers daily. People who are too sophisticated to believe in a devil are captivated by evil in all its forms. Their lives are torn apart into confusing messes, which they then inflict on others with hatred, violence, crime, cruelty, bodily injury, prejudice, ignorance, and many variations of enforced mental and physical suffering. But they do not believe in Satan; to them that belief is folklore meant for children only.

To believe in the reality of Satan does not mean that we posit any physical description of him. The caricature of a red man with beard, horns, tail, and pitchfork is probably far too mild a description for one so evil anyway. Believing in the reality of Satan does mean that we posit the existence of a being who has an intellect and a will, who is evil, whose intention is to bring others into evil and destroy their lives in the ways in which his has been destroyed. It is sad to meet otherwise clear-thinking Christians who cannot run from the reality of evil and yet cannot bring themselves to believe in the person of Satan; they say that evil is an impersonal force without intelligence or destructive intention, merely a reality to be endured. How foolish that must sound to witches and warlocks and other devil-worshiping cultists who have seen and felt in their own lives the tremendous power of the being we call Satan!

How sad it is, also, that we can find this attitude within the Church almost as easily as we can find it outside. People struggle all their lives with problems and find no solution, for they have not been taught that "it is not against human enemies that we have to struggle, but against the Sovereignties and Powers who originate the darkness of this world, the spiritual army of evil in the heavens" (Eph 6:12). Indeed, when we do not see that evil is personal, it becomes difficult to see that it is spiritual at all! It becomes in our minds some kind of cosmic force, more material or, for some, psychological than anything else.

I was confused when the Roman Catholic Church withdrew from her orders of priesthood the order of exorcist. My deep love for and faithfulness to my Church was the source of this reaction, for I saw in it a possible weakening of the understanding of the reality of evil in our world. I am happy that I have received the rite of exorcist, for while I have never used it in a solemn, public exorcism, I have drawn on its power many times in counseling, celebrating the Sacrament of Reconciliation, and praying for healing, for in each of these situations I have had to combat evil.

We need to be aware of the reality and spiritual nature of evil if we are to be able to combat it effectively. Clergy as well as lay people need to be educated in the spiritual realities of our world so that Satan cannot maintain his hold on us. Because many segments of the Church have been fooled by Satan's greatest trick, Satan is free to direct the lives and inner workings of people while a Church too sophisticated to pray for deliverance stands by and watches with little practical help to give.

Deliverance and self-deliverance are important prayers to learn how to pray so that we can deal realistically with the spiritual world and be able to grow spiritually. It is not that we see "a devil around every corner" or that every problem, every illness, is taken care of by deliverance prayer; rather, we merely want to have as one of the tools at our disposal this important prayer, to be used if and when the Lord directs us. It seems that this was the clear intention of Jesus and of the early Church, for we find many references to this kind of prayer in the New Testament, for example, in the words of Jesus before He ascended into heaven: "These are the signs that will be associated with believers: in my name they will cast out devils . . ." (Mk 16:17a). Deliverance prayer, then, is one of the ways we can find freedom for growth in our spirits, minds, and bodies. . . .

Psychologists who have studied the difference between waking and sleeping states of mind tell us that our minds are always working. When we are asleep, they say, we are either dreaming or dealing with dream material; and when we are awake there is a constant flow of images that is just below the threshold of consciousness. These images bring with them moods, desires, anticipations, and feelings, and they can be manipulated, for example, by advertising, to prepare us or urge us to do some particular thing.

Images and pictures have become an important part of our way of life. With television, movies, magazines, and advertising, our minds are bombarded by thousands of images each day.

Some of these images—many more than we would like to admit— become a part of our minds and a part of the way we
think, feel, and act in life.

Our minds are often not ready to deal with the clever
manipulation of images that media present to us because we
have not strengthened our minds with images of God and His
world. Religious imagery, which used to be a large part of the
lives of our forefathers in faith, no longer surrounds us. Where
are the religious artists, musicians, poets, and writers of our age?
Every age before us has had its own share of these talented and
life-giving people, but today we must cherish such a person as
we would a member of a species almost extinct. It used to be in
some cultures that the only themes considered worthy of art
were religious themes. Today, however, many view religious
imagery as so much sentimental piety and dismiss it as patently
irrelevant.

But good religious imagery is neither sentimental nor is it
often pious. When a person dismisses a certain religious image,
what usually irks that person is not the image itself but the style
of the art in which it is depicted, that is, romantic, expressionis-
tic, realistic, abstract; or in music, classical, folk, gospel, jazz,
and so forth. But that which makes an image religious is not the
style of its art but whether or not it puts us in touch with God
Himself, whether it reveals Him to us in new and powerful
dimensions, whether it puts us in touch with the reality He
created. Religious imagery need not be of biblical themes, although the Bible is a rich source for it.

Because religious imagery is that imagery which puts us in
touch with God, Who is all life, all love, mysterious and powerful yet kind and gentle, it gives us life and strength. It frees our
true selves to grow. Religious imagery frees our minds with the
power of holiness that comes from the God with whom it
connects us. That holiness empowers us to ward off the forces of
evil, which are sometimes found in the manipulation and possible destruction that, for example, media images can create.

But without the freeing power of holy images occupying
our minds, we are left open to all the unholy power of the
images thrust on us by advertising and media, for example,

violence, sex, self-centeredness, and the reconciliation of good and evil, that is, the penchant our society has for equalizing good with evil and therefore saying that many things, which in reality are good or evil, are neither good nor evil but value-free. Thus reconciling good and evil results in many common slogans of our modern day such as "If it feels good, do it," "You're not wrong until you get caught," and "You're number one, and you have to grab for all you can in life," none of which make any sense in reference to the life of Jesus or His life in us.

Religious imagery affects our inner selves, strengthening them and bringing about the proper climate for our spiritual growth. Religious imagery is a powerful tool of inner healing prayer. Religious imagery will influence our consciences to make good judgments, will join with our spiritual intuitions to bring us deeply into the spiritual world, and will free our capacity for communion with God so that we will worship Him with greater and greater praise. It will free our spirits and minds to be centered on God, and so to be healthy.

The Task of Freeing Our True Selves

To free our true selves, then, is to yank them out of the seductive values of worldly living. We are not saying that creation is evil or wrong; on the contrary, God created it and loves it for He made it good (Gen 1:1–31 and Jn 3:17), and our job as Christians is to love it and bring its goodness forth (Gen 1:28–29 and Eph 1:9–14).

What we are saying is that reality has a spiritual side, which the materialistic values of our world denies, and it is this denial of reality that leads people into confusion, self-centeredness, and sickness on all levels of being. Freeing our true selves reveals to us the spiritual side of reality and helps us to "see with eyes of faith and hear with ears of faith" so that evil will not win the day or win our lives. When our minds and spirits are freed, we become total human beings and our entire lives will be oriented to the goodness of God. With minds and spirits that are healed and freed we can acknowledge our proper relationship to God and His creation, we can grow spiritually, and we can be made whole.

This part of the book will give us three simple ways to begin this all-important task of becoming spiritually free—a freedom that will come because we will begin to see the world more from God's point of view than from our own. These are not all the possible ways to pray for the freedom of our inner selves, however. It is my hope that these chapters will stimulate the reader to be more aware of this topic and find yet other ways to pray for this kind of freedom. At the very least, I hope that readers will become so familiar with the prayers presented here that they will use them on a regular basis, putting them into language that will be personal and unique to them.

The three ways of praying are these: forgiveness (both giving and receiving it), self-deliverance, and experiencing religious imagery.

Study Guide

1. Do you see it as important to distinguish between mind and spirit? How would you distinguish between the ways these function within you?
2. Is truth primarily an intellectual or a spiritual reality? Explain your answer.
3. How has learning to forgive, or not being able to forgive, affected your spiritual growth?
4. Do you believe that Satan is a personal, spiritual being? Explain the way in which you understand he operates.
5. What advertising images have affected your decisions recently?
6. In what ways do you see a materialistic world view destroying your own spirituality? Making your true self less free?

Suggested Reading

Lewis, C. S. *Out of the Silent Planet*. New York: Macmillan Publishing Co., Inc., 1965.

————, *Perelandra*. New York: Macmillan, 1965.

————, *That Hideous Strength*. New York: Macmillan, 1965.

Nee, Watchman. *The Spiritual Man: Three Volumes*. New York: Christian Fellowship Publishers, Inc., 1968.

Sanford, Agnes. *Behold Your God*. St. Paul, MN: Macalester Park Publishing Co., 1958.

Chapter 5
Forgiveness

As in Chapter 3, we are here approaching a topic about which entire books have been written. Forgiveness is a wide topic because it is so basic to the Christian life. Our goal, then, will not be to cover the topic completely, nor will we attempt to summarize all the good books on the topic. Rather, we will investigate some simple ways to pray for the grace of forgiveness, so that we have a place to begin and a place to which to return when we need to involve forgiveness in our prayers for spiritual growth and inner healing.

We look at forgiveness first as we enter the area of freeing our true selves because that is the proper place for this topic. Forgiving people was central to Jesus' healing ministry, and teaching people to forgive was central to His message of salvation. If we do not experience God's forgiveness of us in our hearts, we do not know what it means to be a child of God, to be loved by Him. Also, if we do not experience God's forgiveness we will not be able to forgive others, for we cannot give what we do not have. We learn how to forgive lovingly, tenderly, and freely by experiencing the way God treats us when we come to Him asking Him to forgive us our wrongdoing.

Many psychologists say that at the heart of the therapy process is the act of forgiving oneself, of coming to accept, understand, and enjoy oneself while at the same time seeing weaknesses, frailties, mistakes, and even sinfulness. But this act of self-forgiveness is basically a religious act; for it is almost impossible to forgive ourselves without God's help, and even if we could forgive ourselves outside of the context of God's forgiveness of us, our self-forgiveness will easily become self-centeredness, and we will be emotionally and spiritually ill again. To forgive, we need God, and when we forgive we free our true selves to grow spiritually.

General Principles

Many individuals have lost the art of forgiving. As I have spoken with people in this situation, I have discovered that rarely have these people ever felt forgiven themselves. The two situations usually go hand in hand, for we usually do to others what has been done to us, in one way or another.

Oftentimes religion, sadly enough, encourages this kind of problem. By emphasizing the seriousness of sin, religion can lay a heavy burden of guilt on people and then not give them a way to lift it. It is true that the Church also preaches the mercy of God, but to find it some people are left with the impression that their contrition must be so complete and their intentions so pure that on a practical level it is not available to them. So they live with sin and guilt as the lot of their lives—they remain in their false selves, and their true selves remain unfree.

Within families a similar pattern often occurs. When an argument takes place, the people involved have their say and maybe even express themselves with violence, verbal or physical, afterward to remain in silence for hours or days. Then after emotions cool down, those people resume communication as though nothing had happened: the issue is never settled, and no forgiveness is offered or accepted.

Another pattern in some families is that some powerful person or persons demand the right to receive an apology but will not receive it graciously. When the offending party asks for forgiveness the simple words "I forgive you" are not said, or, if they are, they are said in such a way and with an inflection of voice that communicates exactly the opposite meaning of the words; rather, the offended powerful person lectures the other on how wrong he was, restates his position again in final victory, or treats the person coldly and unforgivingly. All of this only serves to make the experience of forgiveness bitter and confusing to all involved, thereby inhibiting their spiritual growth.

Therefore, it seems that even the word "forgiveness" is meaningless to many people today, and definitely the actions of forgiveness are not commonly known and practiced. Where people know that they need more than acrimony and bitterness in their lives but cannot bring themselves to real forgiveness, they substitute acceptance or tolerance, but these humanistic virtues are simply inadequate to heal the woundedness that is in us and to bring us into the Kingdom of God where spiritual growth begins.

To forgive people means to restore them to their rightful, and honored place in our hearts. It means to let go of any demand for repayment of hurts suffered. It means to be willing to treat them with kindness, respect, and heartfelt courtesy. It is the free act of people who are in touch with their true selves. None of us can do this alone, especially when we remember Jesus' insistence that we forgive *every* hurt and offense (Mt 18:21–22; Lk 6:27–42); so, finally, to forgive means to pray for the grace of forgiveness from God, Who has first forgiven us.

Many people are under the misapprehension that when we forgive people we condone their actions, or, in other words, we are saying that everything they did was right. Nothing, however, could be further from the truth. For how can we forgive people who are right? No, forgiveness necessarily means that some actual or at least perceived wrong has been done. In forgiving another we acknowledge fully the wrong of those actions and/or the hurt those actions caused. But when we say that our relationship with that person is more important than the hurt we feel, we acknowledge that we ourselves have hurt others just as badly or worse, and in the strength that can only come from Jesus we let go of our bitterness while He heals the hurt, and our true selves are set free.

Forgiveness is necessarily a process, and one that happens according to its own schedule. We cannot force our hearts to do that which they are not yet ready to do. Often we need to wait for the right time and circumstances to forgive a big hurt. In our waiting we ought not to be idle, however. There are several ways in which this process can begin.

Maybe we need to forgive ourselves for being hurt, for taking so long to forgive, or for doing something to someone else similar to what has been done to us. On the other hand, sometimes forgiveness happens in an instant. But Dennis Linn and Matthew Linn, who in their book *Healing Life's Hurts: Healing through the Five Stages of Forgiveness* investigate the nature of the process of healing, say that even in so-called instantaneous forgiveness we often experience each of these five stages (denial, anger, bargaining or conditional forgiveness, depression, and acceptance or unconditional forgiveness), for they are a natural process of healing our wounded selves. Dennis and Matt teach in their book how to pray through each of the five stages and find healing all along the way to the final step, loving forgiveness.

While we talk about forgiveness, we must not overemphasize forgiving others as opposed to being forgiven, because when God forgives us our true selves are freed in some important ways. But to be forgiven is almost as difficult for many as it is to forgive. If we find that statement improbable, let us look at a similar situation: If being forgiven is to be given a gift that we do not deserve, it is similar to being complimented. How many of us feel comfortable when we receive a compliment? Usually our first reaction is not to receive it at all, but rather to deny it. We change the subject, ignore the statement, immediately return the compliment, explain away that for which we have been complimented, or remain silent. And what would be the appropriate response to a compliment, were we to receive it well? I learned the answer to that question on the day of my graduation from college, when I told a teacher how much his course meant to me. He closed his eyes, smiled, nodded his head slowly, and simply said, "Thank you." He accepted my compliment as sincere and allowed it to touch his heart. Any other response reveals our discomfort when we are complimented and shows we find compliments difficult to receive.

If it is difficult for us to receive compliments when we are often at least partially responsible for that which we are being recognized, how much more difficult it is for us to receive forgiveness, which we do not deserve at all! Forgiveness is so difficult for us to accept and believe that God told us once on the Cross that we are forgiven and we spend our entire lives asking Him if He really meant it. It is difficult to believe that anyone could love us that much; or maybe we are so caught up in self-centeredness that we cannot understand what real love is.

Being forgiven is also difficult because it means apologizing, saying we are sorry. And that is difficult to do, of course, because it strikes at our precious pride. How we hate to admit that we are wrong, that we have made a mistake! Of course, we will admit it to ourselves—it would be difficult not to, although we even try that once in awhile—but to admit it to someone else, especially when that Someone is perfect, holy, and has never done anything to hurt us, takes real strength, strength most of us do not have, at least without Jesus at our side, Who often comes to us through the love and prayers of other Christians.

This is one of the reasons that the psychologist Carl Jung praised the Catholic Church for the Sacrament of Reconciliation and said that it kept many people sane and on the road to wholeness: for in that experience we can come to God to ask forgiveness with the aid of another human being. Often it is much easier to believe that God forgives if we know that another human being understands us and is willing to help us along the way. And so when Catholics misuse that Sacrament by celebrating it perfunctorily, or when they ignore it out of a false sense of fear or shame, they abandon something precious and life-giving.

More and more I see Protestant brothers and sisters feeling that same need in their lives and asking their pastors for time for a "confession of soul." Recently at an inner healing service, a fine young man from a Methodist background, who worked for his church and was quite faithful to its practices, came to me at the time for individual ministry because he felt God urging him in his heart to confess the sins of his youth so that he would be entirely healed. After he confessed, we prayed and the grace of God rushed through him to free his entire being. I am not saying here that we cannot go to God on our own and ask Him to forgive us; but I am saying that when we put this request in the context of a human relationship where two or more can pray together in Jesus' name, He is in our midst and can heal us in a powerful way (cf. Mt 18:20), and this is often the very step we need to free us to grow again spiritually.

Finally, we must remember one central truth: Forgiveness is a gift from Jesus, it is a grace. We cannot manufacture it in our hearts. This is one place in which many people stumble in the Christian walk—trying to forgive others in the strength of their own hearts. Because of the destruction that our own sin, original sin, and the sin committed against us have accomplished in our spirits, our human hearts are too petty and hard to forgive. We need the forgiving of Jesus in us. "It is God for his own loving purpose, who puts both the will and the action into you" (Phil 2:13), Paul says; and so even the *desire to forgive* is a gift from Jesus. All we can produce in our hearts is the desire for the desire to forgive; but when we have that and pray with it to God, He begins to work the miracle of forgiveness in us and frees our true selves.

A Description of the Prayer

One simple and powerful way to give and receive forgiveness is to come to Jesus' Cross with our problems. Again, this is not the only way to experience forgiveness, but it is a good place to begin. We are all aware that Jesus forgave our sins when He died on the Cross, yet rarely are we aware of this truth in a moment of crisis—that is, that from the Cross Jesus forgives us in *this* situation, for *this* sin. Instead, the power of the Cross to free our true selves remains dormant while we continue to live in guilt and confusion.

Sometimes we need to pull back from the very real cosmic and universal redemption that Jesus worked on the Cross and look at only one aspect of it, the aspect that applies to us and the problem we are experiencing at this moment. When we do this we are not denying that through the Cross salvation is offered to all people, nor are we trivializing Jesus' suffering; we are only trying to experience His saving Love in a way that will free us from the particular sin of which we are aware at this moment so that we can grow spiritually because of it.

In this prayer we imagine ourselves on Calvary, walking up to the Cross and kneeling at the feet of Jesus. For a moment we allow the meaning of this event to penetrate our hearts. We look at Jesus' wounds, see the blood and perspiration on His body, see the suffering in His eyes; in other words, we allow ourselves to be involved emotionally, intellectually, and spiritually in this scene. Then we see Jesus look directly into our eyes and say, "Father, forgive him, he did not know what he was doing," "Father, forgive her, she did not know what she was doing" (cf. Lk 23:34), and we receive into the depth of our spirits the healing forgiveness of Jesus for us at this moment, in this situation.

Then we imagine the person with whom we need reconciliation approaching Jesus on the Cross, walking up the hill of Calvary, and kneeling down beside us. We see Jesus gently shift His gaze from our eyes to the eyes of this person, and we hear Him say, "Father, forgive him, he did not know what he was doing," "Father, forgive her, she did not know what she was doing," and we realize that the same forgiveness Jesus gives to us He also gives to the person who hurt us. If we are allowing ourselves to experience this scene with our entire beings, our minds are overwhelmed at what He does, our selfishness broken, our pride dashed; our hearts reach out in love.

Then it is our turn to look directly into His eyes and speak the thoughts of our hearts. Whatever we tell Him at this moment, the only requirement is that we are honest about our feelings so that we know He understands us perfectly. Then we acknowledge that His ways are higher than our ways, and we ask that the forgiveness He has for this person flow also through our hearts, that He catch us up in His great act of forgiveness.

When I pray this kind of prayer and share my feelings

honestly with Him, I usually realize how proud and stubborn I
am in relationships. I will often pray something like this:

> *"Lord, how can You do it? How can You love this
> person so completely ... how can You love me? You
> know what we have done to each other, and yet You
> forgive. Jesus, I don't understand it. I don't understand
> how You love and forgive this way. It doesn't make any
> sense at all.*
>
> *"Lord, I don't know what You see to love in this
> other person whom I can't understand. But I do see
> that You love him, and I am shocked and embarrassed
> by Your Love. Jesus, show me what You see in this
> person, show me why You love this person. Catch me
> up in Your great act of loving. I ask that the forgiveness
> that flows from Your heart to him flow through me as
> well. Let me be a part of Your forgiveness. Let me love
> this person with Your Love and forgive with Your
> forgiveness. Thank You, Lord. Amen."*

It is always difficult to pray this prayer and mean every
word sincerely, but the results are worth the pain.

An Example

Once a person came to me who was having great difficulty
in a working relationship. It was the kind of situation in which
it was necessary that he and another man work closely every
day, and what they did affected the lives of many others. The
person who came to me was experiencing intense feelings of
hatred for the other man. As we talked about the situation for
awhile, he realized that he hated the other partly because they
were so much alike. There were also some clear and probably
righteous complaints he had about the way this other man
behaved toward him and the people they served.

As he talked, however, he became convinced that he was the

one who needed to change the more. He realized how his hatred directly contradicted everything he wanted his life to stand for, as well as how it was feeding the destructiveness of the relationship between the two of them. He knew he needed to forgive and to change, for his bitterness was ruining his own spirit. (This is one way we can experience the desire for the desire to forgive mentioned above.)

We prayed the prayer just described. It was an intense experience for the man in which he wept for his sin. With the help of Jesus in prayer, he reached out in love to the other man, whom he now saw as a partner. He spoke to him in the prayer and asked his forgiveness for his hatred and wrongdoing.

Immediately he felt a freedom within his inner self. For the first time in a long while he knew that he was doing what Jesus would do in the situation; indeed, he was doing it *with* Jesus. In turning to Jesus and loving Him enough to love his brother, he began to love himself. This experience was the beginning of his search to find more healing for even deeper problems in his life, for in his reconciliation with himself God freed his true self to grow spiritually. And simultaneously, without his sharing this prayer with the other man, their relationship began to improve and change, so that now each can call the other friend.

This story brings up one sensitive and critical question: When should we go to other people to confess our sin against them and ask forgiveness, and when should we do this in prayer alone or with a third party; and, contrarily, when should we forgive others their sin against us face-to-face, and when should we do it in prayer? We can find the answer to this question by remembering that forgiveness is love, and if we were to give forgiveness or seek it in an unloving way our efforts would be counterproductive.

Therefore, a general rule we can follow is: Forgive another in prayer only; seek forgiveness face-to-face. We forgive others in prayer only because to bring up their faults to them, just so that we could forgive them, is the height of pride and selfishness and therefore is unloving. (All rules have exceptions: One exception to this rule is that in an intimate relationship like a marriage it may be essential, to keep communication open and honest, to tell another of his faults; however, in this situation a good rule to follow is to forgive or at least to work through one's anger before confronting the other.) But we say we are sorry for our sins against others face-to-face with them, because in these situations we have hurt other people and they need our words to be comforted and healed. In being reconciled in this way our pride and selfishness will be broken.

Many have been shocked at this teaching and they attempt to quote the words of Jesus to prove it wrong. However, the words of Jesus read thus: "Therefore, if you are bringing your offering to the altar and there remember that *your brother has something against you,* leave your offering there before the altar, go and be reconciled with your brother first, and then come back and present your offering" (Mt 5:23–24, emphasis mine). This is a Scripture passage often misquoted to read "and there remember that you have something against your brother." But the words of Jesus verify the general rule given above.

Another exception we need to make to the general rule of seeking forgiveness face-to-face is: If the person whom we have offended does not know about our ill feelings toward him, or if sharing our feelings would unduly hurt this person's feelings, then we need to do what we must do in prayer, possibly waiting for the time when it would be appropriate—if that time would ever come—to share our feelings. It is important, however, to be scrupulously honest about whose feelings we are sparing in this situation; in cases like this we always want to be willing to spare the other person's feelings while never sparing our own. In other words, no matter how much it may embarrass us to apologize, as long as by doing so we are not hurting the other person, we must do it. But to share our ill feelings with another when doing so would only hurt that person is tantamount to *using* that person to free ourselves from guilt!

A Sample Prayer

This prayer is only one kind of many different ways to approach forgiveness; it is offered to show how personal and concrete the experience of forgiveness with Jesus can be. Before we pray this prayer, it will be good to review the four steps that were listed in the Preface in the section entitled "A Note on Using the Sample Prayers in This Book." These steps will prepare us for prayer, and when we have completed them we can begin to pray.

> *"Jesus, I thank You for the chance to give and receive forgiveness in a relationship that is a problem to me. I ask Your Spirit to move within me to show me in which relationship in my life You want me to grow spiritually and so to bring before You right now.... Thank You, Holy Spirit, for Your help. Come to me with Your gift of truth so that I will be honest with Jesus and our Father about this relationship.*
>
> *"Spirit of God, I invite You into my imagination. Give me all the gifts I need to pray the perfect prayer You want prayed for me today. Help me to be in the presence of Jesus on the Cross, to walk up the hill of Calvary and to kneel at His feet. I ask You to use my emotions and intuitions to help me understand with my heart and not only my mind what Jesus did for all of us, and for me, on the Cross: His physical suffering ... the rejection He felt ... the pain of having Mary and John with Him ... the struggle within Him to continue loving although He was being tortured unjustly.... Thank You, Holy Spirit, for helping me appreciate in a little way the suffering of Jesus.*
>
> *"Lord Jesus, I see You looking directly into my eyes, and the Love of Your gaze melts my heart. I hear You say, 'Father, forgive him, he did not know what he was doing.' As You say those words my mind cannot believe that they are real! You forgive me? Why ... how ... thank You, Lord. What a gift—a gift I never will deserve! You forgive all my sins, including the sins of bitterness, nurturing grievances, and misuse of anger that I have committed in this troublesome relationship....*

"Now I see the person with whom I am angry coming to You, walking up the hill—just as I did—and kneeling at Your feet—just as I did. You look at him and say, 'Father, forgive him, he did not know what he was doing.'

"Lord, how can You say that to him? He hurt me. Do You mean that this person really didn't know how much damage would be done with his actions and words? Do You mean that this person didn't know, just as I usually don't know how I have hurt others? Do You mean that all of that doesn't matter? Yes, I see You do, for all that matters is that we come to You to be forgiven; all that matters is that You forgive everything for everybody.

"Lord, I honestly do not understand Your attitude, I don't understand how You do it. How can You forgive this person and me and all of us? I know that with my mind I could never understand Yours. So I ask You to let me participate in Your Heart. Let me see this person in the way You do. Let me understand this person's life, hurts, pressures, responsibilities, fears, anxieties—in the same way You do. . . . Let me love this person with Your Love. Let me forgive in Your forgiveness. I ask You, Jesus, to let me be caught up in Your forgiveness just as I would be caught in the currents of a river. Let me allow Your forgiveness to take me wherever it will take me. I abandon myself to You. . . .

"Jesus, Your forgiveness breaks my hardened heart and then heals it. Thank You. Thank You for showing me my own humanness and the humanness of my fellow human being. Thank You for loving us because of and not in spite of our humanness with all its weakness and pettiness. Thank You that I can care again. Thank You that Your Heart now lives in me in this relationship. Lord, teach me to seek this kind of healing in all my relationships.

"Lord, now that You have healed my heart, I ask

You to heal this relationship. You know what to do to make it work again. Direct me to do anything You may want me to do to repair it. I am open to whatever You may ask of me to accomplish Your will for this relationship. I ask only that Your direction be clear, and that You speak to me plainly about that which I must do in a moment of prayer, through the Bible, or in the circumstances of my life. And, of course, I ask for Your help to accomplish what You ask.

"Thank You, Lord Jesus, for Your gift of forgiveness and love. Teach me how to live with Your gift and how to share it with everyone. Let this experience be the first step of a new phase of spiritual growth in my life. Amen."

Study Guide

1. Distinguish between forgiving and excusing. Describe a time in which you have felt completely forgiven. What were your feelings at that time?
2. How were you taught about forgiveness as a child?
3. What difficulties do you experience in trying to forgive another person fully and freely?
4. How do you react to: receiving a gift? receiving a compliment sincerely given? being forgiven for a mistake? being forgiven a wrong you committed consciously and willingly?
5. Under what circumstances is it easier for you to believe that you have been forgiven?
6. What difference have you seen in your life between trying to forgive others or yourself on your own and trying to forgive with God's grace?

Suggested Reading

Dobson, Theodore E. *Inner Healing: God's Great Assurance.* New York: Paulist Press, 1978.

Linn, Dennis, S.J., and Linn, Matthew, S.J., *Healing Life's Hurts.* New York: Paulist Press, 1978.

———, *Healing of Memories.* New York: Paulist Press, 1976.

Sanford, Agnes. *The Healing Light.* Plainfield, N.J.: Logos International, 1978.

Shlemon, Barbara Leahy. *Healing Prayer.* Notre Dame, IN: Ave Maria Press, 1976.

Tapscott, Betty. *Set Free,* Houston, TX: Hunter Books, 1978.

Chapter 6
Self-Deliverance

As has been the case in Chapters 2, 3, and 5, we are here approaching a topic about which many books have been written—deliverance. And again, our aim will not be to summarize them, but rather to see how our knowledge of deliverance can be applied to prayers for inner healing for ourselves, and to see how deliverance can encourage our own spiritual growth.

Deliverance is a new word to some, and an old one to others. Almost everyone associates it with exorcism, and that is a frightening word for most. Those who are familiar with deliverance prayer know that it is a form of exorcism, applied to those cases in which a person is not entirely possessed by an evil spirit but is bothered or "demonized" by one. Moral theology of the Catholic Church distinguishes between exorcism that is solemn (driving out the devil) and simple (curbing the devil's power), and between exorcism that is public (by ministers of and using the authority of the Church) and private (the exorcist acts on his or her own as a redeemed child of God).

Many moralists of this and previous centuries have warned the Church not to forget the duty to use the power of Christ in bringing the world out of evil, and not to dismiss exorcism as one of the tools we would use. They have urged priests celebrating the Sacrament of Reconciliation to exorcise penitents silently in difficult cases, and they have encouraged the laity to use their power in private exorcism. What has come to be known as deliverance prayer is a form of simple exorcism that clergy or laity have the power to pray.

Also, great thinkers in the Church, like St. Alphonsus Liguori, have warned clergy and laity alike not to be too incredulous about the possibility of what they call "demon infestation," and moralists into this century have repeated this instruction. Therefore, we begin this chapter with a premise: Satan is real, intelligent, and evil; he wants to destroy and does infest humans; and Jesus has given the Church the power to be freed of Satan, when the need arises. Thus, prayers for deliverance can be helpful in freeing our true selves to grow spiritually.

General Principles

First and foremost, we need to affirm one principle: There is no "deliverance ministry," only a healing ministry that includes deliverance. Deliverance and healing are two sides of the same coin; deliverance can be described as spiritual surgery, and healing the process of binding together wounds from that surgery or from other sources. Deliverance is to be used together with healing prayer at all times, then, to assist people on their road to spiritual growth and wholeness in Jesus' Love.

This principle comes from the words of Jesus: "When an unclean spirit goes out of a man it goes through waterless country looking for a place to rest, and cannot find one. Then it says, 'I will return to the home I came from.' But on arrival, *finding it unoccupied,* swept and tidied, it then goes off and collects seven other spirits more evil than itself, and they go in and set up house there" (Mt 12:43–45a, emphasis mine). The unoccupied house is the part of the person that has been freed through deliverance prayer but not filled with the Love of God through healing prayer.

Second, while mentioning the power and possible influence of Satan so forthrightly can frighten some people, there is no real need to fear Satan or anything he can do. Jesus has already struggled with him and won; that happened in His death and resurrection and it is an accomplished fact. Therefore, Satan can inflict no lasting harm in one who turns to Jesus for help. Once Satan has been discovered in a person through the gift called discernment of spirits his hours are numbered, for Jesus has given us the authority to drive him out (Mt 10:1; Mk 6:7; Lk 9:1). Furthermore, Jesus is the one who does the actual deliverance, not we. As we praise Him and pray to Him, He in His mercy allows us to experience personally the victory over Satan that He won on the Cross.

Third, we discover the need for deliverance through a spiritual process called discernment of spirits (1 Cor 12:10), not by logic or deduction. This gift is usually experienced as an internal, spontaneous knowledge that a particular person's problems are caused by an evil spirit. While some cases of deliverance follow certain patterns, we cannot generalize too freely from these patterns in an attempt to fit every case with which we come in contact. To do so would be to rely on the flesh rather than the Spirit. The need for deliverance and the deliverance prayer itself are both guided by God when they are authentic. Using the gift of discernment of spirits is the only sure way to know whether a person needs deliverance.

Fourth, we need to note carefully that people who need deliverance have not necessarily—nor usually, in my experience—done something immoral. It is an unfortunately common misconception to think that they have necessarily and voluntarily opened their lives to Satan or invited him into them by doing something gravely immoral. While sometimes this is the case (for example, when a person becomes fascinated with occult powers), often nothing could be further from the truth. People who need deliverance prayer are no more nor less culpable of sin than people who do not. Many times the only reason they need deliverance is that they have suffered—that they bear within them the scars of some kind of physical, psychological, or spiritual trauma. It is through the traumas of our lives that Satan often enters us. Thus we can see why healing prayer and deliverance are needed together to free our true selves.

Fifth, one of the effects of being demonized is that such a person may at times be internally compelled to do evil, immoral, or destructive actions; by being "internally compelled" we mean that their freedom is severely limited or even entirely restricted.

Compulsion to evil or to destruction, especially after healing prayer has been prayed, is one of the signs that deliverance may be necessary. However, we must note that if a person is compelled by psychological or spiritual forces within to do evil, that person's culpability is diminished or even entirely eliminated. Our response to that person's actions, therefore, must not be one of correction and rebuking, but of empathy, sympathy, and kindness—leaving our rebuking for the demon that is infesting the person, and transforming our correction into gentle teaching about remaining free from Satan and living in God's Love after prayer is prayed with or for that person.

Sixth, when we pray for deliverance, we need *not* look for any physical manifestions of release of evil spirits. We will discover that if we want or need to see manifestations for whatever reasons, Satan will sense this and provide them, usually simultaneously diverting us from the real problems that need to be addressed in our prayer. Some have heard that being freed from Satan always involves coughing, sneezing, sighing, yawning, or some other physical expulsion of the demon. People who teach this forget that the process of deliverance is spiritual; sometimes these manifestations are there and need to be endured and sometimes not, and most of the time they can be prevented by prayers to bind the spirits. Similarly, when we pray for deliverance we need not shout or scream or take on a different tone of voice to address Satan. It is our *spiritual authority* to which he responds, and no amount of shouting or screaming will fool him into thinking we have more authority than Christ has given us and we have maintained.

I learned this lesson quite simply several years ago in listening to Agnes Sanford. She spoke of her personal disapproval of bombastic "deliverance ministries" and said that she had found deliverance a simple matter. When she discerned the need for deliverance, she stated, she often did not even bring it up to the person because she was concerned not to embarrass or confuse him, nor did she feel it necessary often even to address the demon straightforwardly. Rather, using the image of Light, she prayed that the Light of God's Love would consume the darkness of whatever problem she discerned and set this person entirely free. In using this prayer myself, I have found it quite adequate in many situations.

Seventh, we need to repeat a statement made in the Introduction to Part II, that we need not be "looking for a demon around every corner" or try to solve every problem we confront with deliverance prayer. Not every problem, not even mental illness, is necessarily caused by demon infestation. On the other hand, being demonized may be a part of the problem that therefore will not yield to other forms of healing prayer. So again we reaffirm the need to enter deliverance using a gift of spiritual discernment, asking Jesus to reveal to us exactly what He wants done so that He can free our true selves to grow spiritually.

A Description of the Prayer

Self-deliverance combined with healing of memories (described in Part III of this book) can be a powerful way to pray when guided by the Holy Spirit. The first people I had ever heard combine these two prayer forms in an integrated way were Rev. Joe Diebels, S.J., and Dolly Ward, R.N., both of whom have worked in the healing ministry for many years. I have met many others since, but it is basically the outline I learned from them which I present here.

First, through the gift of discernment of spirits, we identify the areas that need deliverance. Often they are identified by the sins they tempt us to commit, for example, pride, anger, lust, and so forth, or even by the names of more particiular psycho-spiritual problems, for example, compulsive sexual problems, vanity, death anxiety. While demons often have other names by which they are known, we need to use only one, most of the time, in deliverance prayer. Often it is helpful to write the list of demon-infested areas as it is being revealed in prayer by the Holy Spirit.

Second, we pray prayers of protection from the demons and their companions: We protect our persons, loved ones, and possessions by the Precious Blood of Jesus (this prayer is powerful because it unites us to the victory and salvation Jesus won for us on the Cross); we call on the assistance of Michael the Archangel and the prayers of the saints. We may use blessed salt, blessed oil, or holy water, for often these sacramentals are helpful in breaking Satan's power, for they are material signs of our faith in Jesus' power. We also bind the spirits to be delivered so that they cannot distract us with manifestations. We especially cut them off from communication with other demonic forces around us, and from each other, by asking God to encircle each one with the Blood of Jesus, for example, in a Crown of Thorns (this important point I first learned from Rev. Richard McAlear, O.M.I., and his partner, Mrs. Elizabeth Brennan). In this way we prevent the bound demons within a person from relying on each other or on the strength of unbound companions who have responded to their call for help. Much of the confusion that many people might experience at sessions for deliverance prayer can be totally eliminated with this prayer.

Third, we take our list of evil spirits and, starting with the first and working with only one at a time, we renounce that spirit and cast it out from ourselves. Our prayer can be simple and direct: "In the name of Jesus Christ of Nazareth, I renounce you, demon of _____ , and I cast you out of me and away from me into the hands of Jesus, Who will do with you as He wills." This prayer, prayed sincerely, will loosen the demon's grasp on us, leaving him no reason to stay and giving him every reason to leave. We deepen the effect of our word of command by praising Jesus and asking Him to deliver us.

Fourth, we ask the Holy Spirit to stir our memories and reveal to us any time that this particular demon had control of us and led us into sinful or destructive thinking, feeling, or behavior. We wait, then, for the Spirit to reveal the times in which this spirit has influenced our lives, and we will probably be surprised at all the forgotten and repressed memories that come forth.

Fifth, with each of the events that the Spirit reveals, we pray a prayer for healing of memories (more fully discussed in Part Three), thus asking Jesus to "occupy the house" (cf. Mt

12:44) that the demon used to inhabit. In this way God comes to dwell where the evil spirit used to be, and so we become a little more God's own in actuality as well as intention. In healing of memories, then, we ask Jesus to show us how He was with us when this particular event was occurring, and we accept into our hearts the love He was trying to give us when we were hurt. Thus we use the freedom God has given us to promote our spiritual growth.

Sixth, after the healing of memories for the first area of concern has been completed, we continue our prayer, moving to the second area on our list, repeating steps three, four, and five for each area of need until we work our way through the entire list we received in discernment.

Seventh, we pray a prayer of peace for ourselves and for the place in which we have prayed. We ask the Holy Spirit to be in charge of our inner beings, calming all the areas of ourselves that have been touched in this prayer, bringing them into harmony with each other, with the other parts of ourselves, and with Jesus. We ask the Spirit to guard these newly healed parts of us from people and situations that would disturb the healing until it has firmly taken root. We also pray a prayer of blessing for the place in which we have prayed, asking the Spirit to cleanse it of all companion evil spirits, filling it with Light and Love.

It is important to note that people who have been involved seriously in occult practices find themselves in a unique situation. Because of the seriousness of the occult world, and because of the power of the evil spirits who control it, they may find themselves defeated whenever they try to pray for self-deliverance. These people need to seek help from a competent minister of healing and deliverance, and they can be confident that Jesus will free them through this means.

When we have spiritually discerned the need for this kind of self-deliverance/inner healing prayer, we often need to pray in this way for several weeks, either daily or every other day at first, then decreasing the frequency as we are led by the Spirit, until, by not prompting us to pray in this way, He reveals to us that we no longer need this prayer. The repetition is important not because the first command of deliverance did not have its spiritual effect, but because a demon once removed will try to find his way back into us (cf. Mt. 12:43–45). We must attack his counterattack or we run the risk of being defeated by his subtle ways.

Another reason for the repetition is to reassure ourselves psychologically that we are free. When we are delivered and Satan cannot reenter us, he often attempts to make us think he has reentered us by various temptations to do those very things for which we sought freedom through deliverance. The repetition of the prayer, along with a renewal of traditional Christian practices like reading Scripture, receiving the Sacraments, and leading a moral life, renews our own awareness of Jesus' total control of the situation. We cannot overemphasize the importance of this component of the process of healing combined with deliverance.

Again, we continue to pray in this manner for several weeks because of the healing of memories involved. As we pray each day about the same problem areas, new memories will arise to be healed. In this way we are strengthening ourselves against Satan's further attacks, for we are allowing Jesus to heal our problems to the tips of their very roots. Healing of memories allows Jesus to enter our personalities and spirits part by part, strengthening us in holiness against the onslaught of evil. Thus praying in this fashion for several weeks as the Spirit guides us can bring great freedom for our inner selves and lead to much spiritual growth.

An Example

I myself used this prayer to be freed from fear and from bitterness several years ago after I first met Joe and Dolly. The fear from which I needed healing was a fear of growing up that I knew had begun in me when I was quite small, so I knew that it was deep-rooted, and I knew that there were many memories that needed to be brought into the Light of God's healing Love. Similarly, the bitterness from which I needed healing was from my own reaction to being adopted, for as a child I had decided to interpret that event primarily as a rejection by my natural parents, and so I was bitter toward them.

I used the method of praying described above. Joe and Dolly had helped me discern my areas of need (it is not a bad idea in cases like this to get a second or corroborating opinion from some trusted spiritual adviser or friend), and so I proceeded to use this list of concerns as the basis of my daily prayer for awhile. I found especially freeing the healing of memories part of the prayer, for many deeply hidden and long-forgotten memories came to light—times in which I felt guilty because of my fear, times in which fear drew me into deper fear and finally into anxiety and depression, times in which bitterness seemed to control me and pollute relationships in which I then needed to ask forgiveness (Chapter 5), times in which I accepted my bitterness as part of my personality and therefore saw myself as less a human being (accepting my false self) because of it. All these memories needed to be healed; and I found to my great surprise—because Love is always a surprise—that God wanted to heal them both to make me happy and to make me a more effective servant for Him and His Kingdom.

I found great release as I prayed for each area of concern on my own. And once I had been completely freed and I no longer found the Holy Spirit directing me to pray these prayers, I found it was not at all difficult to be open rather than defensive, to be understanding rather than bitter, to respond to God's gift of Joy rather than to be anxious and depressed, although I found that these new responses to life developed slowly over a period of time. Furthermore, in retrospect I began to see that what I and others had identified as stubbornness in my personality was really the stubbornness of the spirits that had been infesting me. Also, with some work, a few apologies, and some prayer, most of the relationships that had been marred by fear and bitterness consequently improved. Jesus had helped me grow spiritually and had freed my true self, not only through these prayers, but also by the ways they enabled me to live differently.

A Sample Prayer

Before we begin to pray this prayer we need to have before us a list of the areas in which, through the gift of discernment of spirits, we know we need deliverance. Discernment is often not a process that happens in an instant or in a short period of time. It comes quite often after many days, even weeks, of prayer and searching for answers to the questions of our lives. As mentioned above as well, it often comes in conjunction with discussion with a trusted spiritual adviser or friend. We do need to pray simply and ask the Spirit to guide us to know whether we need deliverance prayer, and, if we do, to know in which areas we need it.

Also, more than with other kinds of inner healing prayer, there is a right time and wrong time to pray for deliverance. It is important to be extremely sensitive to our inner needs and to the guidance of the Holy Spirit in choosing a time in which we pray this prayer, *for praying for deliverance when we are not prepared for it will lead to failure and consequent disappointment, and may in some cases lead to psychological and spiritual damage within us.* So let us listen closely to the Spirit right now: Maybe He is urging us gently to pray this prayer at this moment, maybe He is cautioning us to wait. *We must not proceed* before we have some kind of notion of what the Spirit sees as best for us at this time and in these circumstances.

Further, if we are not at all familiar with healing of memories, before we pray this prayer reading Part Three of this book will be helpful, if not essential; for healing of memories, we remember, is at the heart of healthy deliverance prayer. Learning how to pray for healing of memories will prepare us to pray for deliverance effectively.

If we *spiritually discern* that this is a proper time for us to pray deliverance prayer, and *if* we have with us the results of our discernment, that is, a list of problem areas that the Spirit has revealed to us are areas of demon infestation, and if we have a spiritual confidence that this is a need for which we can pray alone and do not need the assistance of someone else who would pray with and for us, we need then to prepare ourselves for this prayer by reviewing the four steps outlined in the Preface in the section entitled "A Note on Using the Sample Prayers in This Book." After we have completed these preparations, we can begin to pray.

> *"Thank You, Lord, for showing me that I need this prayer now, and for showing me the areas of my life in which You desire to free my true self through deliverance and healing of memories so that I can grow spiritually. I walk into this experience holding Your hand, Jesus, trusting in Your victory over Satan on the Cross and on Easter Sunday morning. Because I have been baptized into You and am a part of Your body, I too share in that victory and claim its power to free me right now.*
>
> *"So, Jesus, I ask the protection of Your Precious Blood, shed in love for all of us and for me, for the forgiveness of our sins and for our freedom from any and all bondage to Satan, on me, my loved ones, and my possessions. I ask for the prayers and protection of Mary, my Mother. Further, I ask You to send to my assistance all the heavenly hosts of angels led by Michael the Archangel, for they continue to fight Satan to this very day. Please ask all the saints with You to pray with me now that I may be free."*

Next we pray asking Jesus to bind the demons within us from any sound or movement, from any spiritual, psychological, or physical activity, naming and binding each one separately. Then we ask Him to surround each of them with a crown of thorns, and with His own Precious Blood to cut them off from communication with each other and with any other spirits from whom they may wish to draw power, or with whom they may wish to consort in any way. Again we name each evil spirit individually, surrounding it with Jesus' Blood.

> *"Now, Jesus, I ask You to renew the presence of Your Spirit within me that I may pray with simple and*

fervent faith, hope, and love. Give me the courage to do what I must do. In the name of Jesus Christ of Nazareth in Whom I live and Who stands with me now, I renounce you, demon of _____, and I cast you out of me and away from me into the hands of Jesus, Who will do with you as He wills. *Thank You, Jesus, for the freedom You win for me. . . ."*

We continue to praise Jesus for a while, asking Him to deliver us. Then we begin the second half of our prayer, our request for healing of memories.

"Now, Spirit of God, I invite You into the depth of my heart, into my memory both conscious and unconscious, to bring forth any account of an event in which this demon influenced my life, which You want healed at this time. Let me spend some moments of quiet with You waiting for these memories to be revealed. . . . As they come forth, Jesus, help me to see You in those situations with me, loving me, guiding me, offering me Your help and assistance. Heal within me that part of my personality or spirit that was damaged. Soothe the woundedness of that moment with the ointment of your gentleness and kindness, and plant Yourself firmly in that part of my life. Bring Your Light into that part of me that has been dark and confusing, contributing to all kinds of pain in my life. Thank You, Jesus, that You are a healer, and that You take the time to heal me."

As we continue to pray, we allow Jesus to heal all the memories His Spirit brings forth, and we do not rush this process, for it is extremely important to deliverance prayer. Once we sense that each memory that has been brought forth has also been healed, we repeat the previous two paragraphs of the prayer, this time moving on to the next area of concern on our list. We take the time to move slowly through each area, making sure we do all that God wants us to do at this time. Finally, when we are finished with all the areas, we can conclude.

> *"Thank You, Lord, for all that You have done for me. I now ask You to grant me Your gift of peace throughout my entire being. I ask You to send the Light of Your Love into my inner self to calm all the areas of my life that have been touched by Your power. Please bring them all into harmony with each other, with all the other parts of myself, and, most importantly, with You. I ask You to wrap around me a cloak of Your protection, especially to guard all these sensitive areas from any people or situations that would undo what You have begun. Let this healing take firm root within me, Lord, before it is tested. Thank You.*
>
> *"I also ask You to bless this place in which I have prayed. Send Your Spirit through it as Light to brighten it and as Breath to cleanse it of all spirits that do not confess You as their Lord. Let all who enter this place receive a blessing of peace and joy. Thank You, Jesus, for being willing and able to set all things straight. Teach me now how to use my true self, which You have freed, not only for my own spiritual growth, but also for building Your Kingdom in the world. Amen."*

Study Guide

1. What thoughts and feelings come to mind with the word *deliverance?* What is your attitude toward the reality and effectiveness of deliverance as a means of spiritual growth?
2. What is the necessary relationship among deliverance, healing, and spiritual growth?
3. Describe your feelings about the possibility of needing deliverance in order to let Jesus free your true self.
4. Why do you think Satan seems to affect so much of this world if Jesus has won the victory over him on the Cross?

5. Do you see a connection between being delivered of demons and freeing your true self? Explain.

Suggested Reading

MacNutt, Francis. *Healing*. Notre Dame, IN: Ave Maria Press, 1974.

Scanlon, Michael. *Deliverance, Freedom from Evil Spirits*. Ann Arbor, MI: Servant Publications, 1980.

Stapleton, Ruth Carter. *The Gift of Inner Healing*.

Tapscott, Betty. *Set Free*. Houston, TX: Hunter Books, 1978.

Chapter 7
Religious Imagery

Since the French Enlightenment, thinking in the Western world, both secular and religious, has had a tendency to separate too far the rational from the imaginative and spiritual. One reason for this situation is the influence of certain philosophical movements that suggest we need to view reality objectively and rationally in order to reflect on life in a valid way. When we begin to live our lives from an objective and *entirely* rational point of view, however, we are in danger of losing touch with some extremely important dimensions of our being—imagination and spirit.

Yet it seems that, because our Western civilization is utilitarian and materialistic and therefore tends not to understand the imaginative and spiritual realities of life, instead preferring the objective and rational, common people in our society have been taught to approach life mostly as a material endeavor when it is indeed that, but also much more than that.

Similarly, during the Enlightenment, the French Rationalists found many reasons to attack religion because of its then unscientific points of view on many issues of concern to humankind. Many sectors of the Church have responded to these attacks—which to some measure continue into our day in different forms—by trying to prove that religious thought is rational and empirical. While to a certain extent this rebuttal was needed both for internal Church reform and for our intellectual relationship with the world, in certain areas it seems that the Church all but abandoned its own rich heritage of imaginative and even spiritual wisdom, just to prove how rational it could be.

One such area is religious imagery, one of the greatest sources of imaginative and spiritual wisdom in the Church. For too long in the Western Church we have related to religious images in an objective way—looking at them, using them in a kind of saccharine piety, analyzing them, but not experiencing them. If, however, we are to find the depth of spiritual wisdom in this, one of the Church's greatest treasures, we need to experience it, not only look at it or analyze it. When we pray in this way with religious imagery it will contribute to our spiritual growth.

General Principles

Images exist to be experienced, that is, felt, cherished, allowed to become a part of our lives. Images are nonrational modes of thought, often expressed in few words or no words at all, that gather for us our perceptions, deep emotions, long-felt hopes, dreams, and fears in order to help us interpret reality as we live it. An example is "family"—we need no other words for this image to be real and communicate to us. Similarly, *Christian religious* images accomplish all of the above and more, for they are a medium through which God touches us, and through them He reveals to us His Life and Love. Therefore, they gather for us our deepest impressions of God and the hopes, dreams, and fears within us concerning our relationship with Him.

When we make religious imagery ours, when we allow it to become personal, we are experiencing it. Experiencing religious imagery has several effects. First, it makes us eminently aware of the fact that God is both awesome and friendly, both totally other than us yet able to be one with us, both the Creator of a vast and unimaginable universe and the pursuer of our spirits; we grow spiritually as we discover through religious imagery Who God really is. Second, it gives us a new point of view concerning the reality in which we live, for in religious imagery is the power to change the way we think, feel, and act, because the power of God is in it and because it activates the creative forces of our minds, thus freeing our true selves. Third, through religious imagery we come to integrate opposites within our perception (thus our true selves are freed in another way), for it is the role of the intellect to separate and evaluate, but it is the role of the imagination—the home of imagery—to unite, rearrange, and bring together.

In understanding the importance of looking at life through more than rational eyes, the words of St. Bonaventure (1217–1274) are helpful. In the prologue of *The Soul's Journey Into God* (Paulist Press, 1978), he warns us *not* to believe that "reading is sufficient without unction, speculation without devotion, investigations without wonder, observation without joy, work without piety, knowledge without love, understanding without humility, endeavor without divine grace, reflection ... without divinely inspired wisdom" (pp. 55–56). Religious imagery accomplishes this task by uniting these opposites so that we can more clearly see reality as it is, thus leading us to closer contact with its Creator.

The first place we can look to discover religious imagery is in religious art. Good art is not merely an object of beauty that we admire from a distance, but rather it calls from us a personal response—an emotion, a perception, an understanding—that brings a person into new wisdom and therefore contributes to that person's spiritual growth.

In this sense, the icons of the Eastern Christian churches are the paradigm of true religious art and imagery. For icons are not brought into existence like any other kind of art. First of all, icons are most often painted by monks whose lives are given to God in prayer and love. When a monk is going to paint an icon, he prepares by spending weeks in fasting and prayer, so that he will be more deeply in touch with God and the spiritual world. After this great spiritual discipline, practiced to contact that which he wishes to portray in art, he paints his icon as a window into that spiritual world for anyone who would pray before it desiring to see. This is the true meaning of spiritual imagery—a window into the spiritual world for those who look and listen with faith. This is also the rationale behind all religious art, and so we can see how good religious art satisfies a deep human need.

As we mentioned in the Introduction to Part Two, our unconscious minds live night and day in a constant stream of images; it is from this stream that our dreams come at night, but these images also continue to flow all day long just beneath the threshold of our consciousness. When we daydream we are beginning to enter this realm of images; when we begin to fall asleep, we also notice that these images often flood our minds. And so we see that image-making is part of the nature of the human mind, that is, it is part of human nature.

Our minds, then, need images and use them at an unconscious level whether or not we relate to images consciously or care about them. In other words, we cannot stop our minds from making images just because they are not important to our conscious ways of thinking. If our minds are image-hungry, if they are constantly producing images and bringing in images from our surroundings, it would contribute to freeing our true selves if they were fed on wholesome and holy images. Religious imagery fills that need. However, we have already noticed that our civilization and even segments of our churches do not understand, appreciate, or use religious imagery. And, in general, each of us as an individual has not been taught to appreciate and use religious imagery for our spiritual growth.

The result is that our image-hungry minds are welcoming into them the images that society and media thrust at them every day—images of sex, violence, self-centeredness, and reconciling good and evil. When we do not strengthen our true selves on the food of religious imagery, these kinds of images are all we leave for our minds to feed on. If we do not strengthen ourselves against the values of a secular and nonbelieving world contained in the images thrust at us daily, we will necessarily be drawn into that world, or at least have a difficult time fighting its power, and so unwittingly reinforce our false selves.

Another sad result of not feeding our minds on religious imagery comes from the relationship between the images in our minds and the thoughts, feelings, and actions that direct our lives. To understand this relationship, we can analyze television commercials, whose sole objective is to stimulate the viewer to think, feel, and act to buy certain products. In analyzing commercials it is important to note how much is communicated to the viewer in logic, and how much is communicated in pictures and song (i.e., images) and in words that draw pictures or create comparisons and inferences.

As we analyze most television commercials we will find many, many digressions from logic; but it is not important in a commercial to be logical, for the real message in a commercial is not in the logic, it is in the images. Commercials in general do not tell us that it is logical that we should buy something—for many times it is not logical, or logic makes no difference in the sale—but rather we are told we will have prestige, sex appeal, a happy and carefree life, or the total solution to our problems if we buy a particular product. And this message is communicated in images: The girl gets her boyfriend because she uses a particular product; a homemaker is free from duties because she uses another kind of product; a third product promises—in images only—to make the person who uses it sexually desirable and even successful in sexual "conquests."

Companies spend millions of dollars advertising their products in this fashion—because it works. These images influence large numbers of people to buy the products, and they make these people feel better just because they have that product. Images strongly influence our decisions, our thoughts, and our feelings. Further, some research has been done in "subliminal advertising," that is, hiding images that will influence the minds of the public in the midst of nonadvertising pictures. The most famous study was one in which a movie frame depicting a box of popcorn was spliced in between the frames of a feature film at a theater; those there didn't know they saw the picture of the popcorn, it sped by so quickly, but within five minutes the lobby was filled with people wanting to buy popcorn.

If these kinds of images influence us to buy the products that are so advertised, can we allow our minds to speculate for a moment on the power of media images, or of religious images, to form our values and to influence our more important decisions and actions? The consequences of the answer to this question can be overwhelming.

If our minds are not filled with God—if they are not filled with holy thoughts and images—they will be filled with other kinds of images that will lead to unholy thinking, feeling, and behavior. It is not just a simple pious practice but it is all-important for the freedom of our true selves and for our spiritual growth to fill our minds with holy and religious imagery, to strengthen our minds against the manipulation of an atheistic and secular world.

A Description of the Prayer

As we saw above, experiencing religious imagery means making it our own, making it personal. So very often we have heard various truths about our faith, never allowing them to have any effect on us, that is, never becoming personally involved in them, never caring about them. Thus these truths remain abstract for us and do not become life-giving, as they were meant to be. Experiencing religious imagery can change all of that, so that these truths can contribute on a daily basis to our spiritual growth.

One could never list all the possible Christian religious images because certain images bring some people close to God but are meaningless to others. But we can say that religious images are not necessarily from the Bible, although the Bible is a rich source for them; neither do they always involve Jesus, the Father, the Spirit, or some religious personage, although they often do. We do not "make an image religious" by using God or Jesus in an image as a mental tool. Rather, an image is religious in itself and by its own nature when it reveals the depth of God's awesomeness and Love to us. Some images to which many people respond are: the Heart of Jesus, the Messiah as Suffering Servant, God's family (the Trinity, the Holy Family, the Church), the Body of Christ, Jesus' Precious Blood, the Good Shepherd, Living Water, the Light of God, the Tree of

Life, the New Jerusalem, and various images from the parables and from the stories of the life of Jesus.

We experience one of these images, then, by personalizing it. We ask ourselves how we think about it, what we feel about it, what associations we already have with it. We try to make it concrete for ourselves by allowing ourselves to be a part of it. In doing this we are not trivializing the image or the reality it represents; we are only finding our relationship to it. Once we make this initial step into the image, it will begin to carry us deeper and deeper within it and within God, suggesting further responses we want to make, suggesting choices for our prayer and for our living, suggesting new appreciation of God in His relationship to us.

In this sense, the prayer is quite simple. We do not *do* much in it; it carries itself and us along. As it carries us we will want to be especially aware of all our emotions and unique responses to the prayer. Maybe we will want to journalize about it (Chapter 3), or it may suggest to us to walk down one of several other forms of prayer already discussed in these pages, for example, integrating opposites within us (Chapter 4), or the need for forgiveness prayer (Chapter 5), or healing of memories (Part Three). In this way, we use praying with images as part of a larger prayer form. Remembering that we are experiencing the image for our spiritual growth, that is, to come closer to the God with Whom it is supposed to put us in contact, we follow the leadings we sense in the Spirit once this prayer has begun.

Some people have difficulty keeping their minds focused on an image for a period of time, and others have the related problem of finding that, when they pray with images, the images seem to become bizarre and unrelated to the religious purpose at hand. Both of these problems come because we have not been taught how to think in images from our youth, and so our minds do not have the discipline necessary to do it well. There are two possible approaches to solving this problem.

One is to pray to cleanse and rededicate our imaginations to God (Chapter 1) as a way of giving more control over our inner selves to God; in this kind of praying we should not exclude prayer to cleanse our intellects and wills as well. These kinds of prayers will calm our minds under the gentle power of the Holy Spirit. The other approach is practice and repetition; we cannot learn anything worthwhile without our share of failure, recommitment, and repetition.

An Example

Once a young man came to me for help because he was depressed and ready to leave school. After taking the time to understand his feelings and to feel them with him, I realized that he felt lonely, rootless, and therefore insecure. He felt as if no one cared for him as the most important person in life; he did not feel special, needed, or wanted to any intense degree. He lacked a sense of his own personal worth, because his own father (from whom a son derives his masculine identity) was a weak and indecisive man.

As we talked, I heard within me the voice of the Father calling to him, and so when the time for prayer came, I prayed a prayer to help him relate to the family of God so that it could be his own family as well. For even though we call God our Father frequently and even daily, we often do so without feeling His fatherly pride in us, without availing ourselves of His understanding and fatherly guidance, without feeling His intense fatherly Love. Because we have approached this image too rationally, it has become abstract and therefore devoid of feeling and also meaning. Our Father-child relationship with God often needs to be liberated within us, whether we see ourselves as a small child or as an adult child whose Father is God.

And so in prayer we recreated the scene of his birth, but we saw him being born into God's family as well as into his human family. We imagined what had always been true: the Father cradling him in His arms with great pride and joy in His eyes over His new son, speaking to him words of commitment and saying they would be together for all of his life, filling His son with a deep sense of identity that comes from knowing Who his Father is and how much He loves him.

We continued prayer, seeing Mary who, through the power

of her Son's resurrection, was able to mother him, teaching him about the world, cuddling and protecting him, allowing the softness of her caresses and the strength of her spirit to saturate him with good feelings about himself and the life he lived. And we saw Jesus brothering him, teaching him about the world, about himself, and about nature, playing with him, protecting him from dangers, and letting him sit on His lap to tell Him all his problems and joys.

The prayer seems amazingly simple, almost childlike; but then again, the young man needed to know how much he was a child—a child of God and a member of His intimate family circle. The prayer greatly strengthened the young man; indeed, it was the beginning of a new phase of spiritual growth in his life. Hope began to stir within him so that slowly he began to find his place in life and shake his depression. He was able to remain in school, and, by praying himself in a similar way, he came to believe in his spiritual family and to rely on their Love for him. In that Love he began to find who he was (his true self) and to feel at home with himself.

A Sample Prayer

Before we pray this prayer, especially if we have not prayed this way all that much in the past, it might be important to return to Chapter 1, "Cleansing the Imagination, Intellect, and Will," and to pray the Sample Prayer that concludes that chapter. Doing this will help to free our imaginations and bring them more under the control of the Holy Spirit, thus liberating them greatly from a tendency to wander or to create unwieldy images. It will also rededicate our imaginations to God, and it will therefore make them more open to following a flow of images under His guidance.

When we sense that we are ready to pray this kind of prayer, we need to prepare ourselves to pray by going through the four steps mentioned in the Preface under the heading "A Note on Using the Sample Prayers in This Book." Having completed these preparatory steps, we can begin to pray. The image on which we will focus in this prayer is our spiritual family.

> *"Thank You, Jesus, for all the ways in which You love me and help me to grow. Today I thank You especially for teaching me that God is my Father. With that one word You have opened for me an entirely new world, a world in which the Creator is also my Father, Who provides for me a family in Himself, in You, and in Your mother. Thank You, Jesus, that through this prayer You will begin to heal all the ways in which I have found my own experience of my human family to be needing something more.*
>
> *"Lord, I ask You to send Your Spirit within my imagination to help me with this prayer. Reveal to me through this prayer Your own heart and the feelings that You as a human being have for me. Release within me, also, my ability to respond to our Father and to Mary as my spiritual parents.*
>
> *"Spirit of God, I ask You to help me imagine myself as a newborn baby in the arms of God my Father. Let me feel the strength of His arms holding me and protecting me, let me take into my deepest self the security that comes from His embrace. . . . As I feel the passion of His Love for me, help me to respond to it naturally. Let me look into His eyes and see the pride He has in me and the kindness He feels for me. . . . Let me hear Him speak to me: 'You are My child, and I love you. I have given you life, and with life comes My Love. You can do nothing that I will not forgive. When you need Me, know that I will be with you—not that I might be, but that I will be. You can trust Me because I am your Father, and I care about what happens to you.' "*

If at this point a memory comes to our minds of a time as a small child or as an adult in which we did not think that our Father was with us when we needed Him, let us stay with that memory for awhile, allowing ourselves to feel our Father's loving and caring in the midst of that difficulty.

> *"Spirit of God, give me the grace of forgiveness for my human father for all the times I needed him and he wasn't there. Help me to let go of all my defensiveness toward him, now that my Father God is taking his rightful place in my life. Thank You, Lord, for this grace. . . .*
>
> *"I thank You, Lord, that I see my Father giving me as a newborn baby to my mother Mary, who, through the power of her Son's resurrection, is able to be my mother as well. Thank You that I can have a spiritual mother to help me as only a mother can.*
>
> *"Let me feel her caress. Let me see the depth of wonder and interest in her eyes as she looks at me; it seems as if she fully knows my spirit, and she loves what she sees. . . . Let me know that I can spend time with her, that she has all the time in the world for me. Release within me a sense of abandon that I can feel the security that she can give me because her Son gives it to her. . . . Let me hear the gentleness and strength of her voice as she speaks: 'You are my child, and I will always care for you. I will always be with you to mother you and give you what you need. Let me teach you what my Son has taught me about life, and let me share with you the mysteries of the universe that He has shared with me. Whenever you need me, look for me, call me, I cannot be far away, for I love you.' "*

If, at this point, a memory comes to our minds of a time as a small child or as an adult when we felt lonely and motherless, let us spend a time in that memory now, allowing the Love of God to flow into us through Mary and heal that wound.

> *"Holy Spirit, help me to forgive my human mother all her shortcomings, especially now that I know the*

wounds they left in me can be healed through the love of my spiritual mother, Mary. Thank You for that grace. . . .

"Thank You, Lord, that I see myself also with Jesus, my older brother. How His size and confidence give me security! How His presence gives me a sense of knowing who I am! Thank You, Jesus, for coming into my life to be my companion. . . . I want to learn from You, Jesus, about the meaning of my life.

"Holy Spirit, help me now to listen to Jesus: 'Come with Me; I am your Brother. There are many things I must show you. Take My hand and let Me show you all about the world in which we live. Let Me reveal yourself to you. Let Me teach you about nature, about other people, about how to live in this world that the Father and Spirit and I have created. Let Me be your Guide and your Friend; I will never fail you, and I will even make sure that we have some enjoyment along the way. Always know that you can come to Me, for I am your Brother, willing and able to help you in all things. Trust Me, for I love you.' "

If a time of deep confusion comes from our memories now, let us stay with that memory, allowing the security that Jesus brings to us to heal the pain of that experience, as we realize that He was with us then, even if we did not know it.

"Thank You, Holy Spirit, for helping me in this prayer to know my spiritual family and to grow in my love for those who so deeply love me. Let the grace of this healing moment penetrate into the depth of my being and set my true self free, in the security of knowing that I am a special member of God's intimate family circle. Fill my heart with all the love that my human family could not, for whatever reason, give to me, so that I can love as Jesus calls me to love. Amen."

Study Guide

1. What are some of your favorite religious images? How is this imagery a personal experience for you? How has this imagery encouraged your spiritual growth?
2. How does religious imagery draw you into the spiritual world?
3. How do secular images, such as the ones you receive from media and advertising, affect the way you think, feel, and act?
4. What experience have you had in using religious imagery in prayer? How has praying in this way affected your spiritual growth?
5. Recall an experience in which an abstract religious truth suddenly became personal to you. What feelings arose in you during this experience? How has it freed you to express your true self?

Suggested Reading

Lewis, C. S. *The Chronicles of Narnia.* New York: Macmillan Publishing Co., Inc., 1970, seven vols.

Progoff, Ira. *At a Journal Workshop.* New York: Dialogue House Library, 1975.

Sanford, John. *The Kingdom Within.* Ramsey, NJ: Paulist Press, 1980.

Part Three

Healing of Memories

Introduction
We Ask Christ to
Renew Our Memories

"Your mind must be renewed by a spiritual revolution so that you can put on the new self that has been created in God's way, in the goodness and holiness of the truth" (Eph 4:23).

Healing Our Personal Histories

Healing of memories is probably the most popular form of inner healing today. More people have experienced spiritual growth through prayers for the healing of memories than through any other kind of inner healing prayer. And that is for a good reason: Many of our present-day problems began a long time ago in an event or in a series of events that have left an indelible mark on our psyches.

It has been the various schools of psychology that have made us aware of the effect of our past on our present. But so very often, as we live our lives meeting various struggles over and over again, we do not or cannot take the time to remember when it all began and "get to the root of the problem." We condemn ourselves for our behavior, while often this behavior began only after someone else did something similar to us, or only after we endured some trauma to which our present behavior seems to be a type of remedy.

There is, then, a delicate balance between being responsible for our present behavior on the one hand, and looking for the root cause of our behavior in some trauma we have endured on the other. It is necessary to be aware of both these aspects of a situation for healing of memories to take place. For when we do not claim responsibility for our present actions, attitudes, and feelings, we are saying we are the victims of fate. While this point of view may be a palliative for our consciences, it leaves us no hope (and therefore cannot be Christian); for hope is present only when there is a possibility of change, and fate allows for little or no change or growth.

When we take responsibility for our present situation we acknowledge that to an extent we have chosen it. Somehow our depression, anger, confusion, or personality and relationship disorders serve some need within us; otherwise they would not be there. We are not entirely victims of fate, but we have chosen our situation and we have chosen incorrectly. This may seem to be a harsh statement and it may be difficult for us to admit, but only when we acknowledge our incorrect choice can we then see new alternatives and choose correctly. If we live as if we were victims of fate we have no control over our futures, but if we have free will we can decide to undo bad choices from the past with a new choice aiming our lives more accurately toward Jesus and His Gospel, that is, toward spiritual growth.

To live in a world of fate where we are only victims of what happens to us is to live without free will. We cannot have it both ways, that is, we cannot say that life has dealt us a poor hand of cards and there is nothing we can do about it, while also saying we are created by God with dignity and are worth healing!

However, not everything that happens to us in life is a result of our own choice alone. Some things are the results of the choices of others; some the result of sin, temptation, and evil; and some the result of the events of history. It is for these aspects of a situation that we need Jesus' healing comfort.

On the other hand, while we do not choose these things to happen, we do choose our responses to them. If we were to place ten different people in the same situation they would react to it in ten different ways. When we react in the unique way in which we do, we must recall that there were many other ways in which we could have responded, but we did not choose any of them; we chose our own way, and so we are responsible for it. In other words, eight-year-old Johnny's mother can tie his shoes for him; but, if she is to do that, he has to let her! And he has made his choice not to grow.

We look extensively at the issue of freedom of choice as we begin to examine healing of memories because, to a great extent, healing of memories is a rechoosing of our past. In healing of memories we choose to relive our memories as they *really* happened. Because "Jesus Christ is the same today as he was yesterday and he will be forever" (Heb 13:8), we see how His Love was always available to us, even in those times in which we were not able to feel it. As we begin to see our personal past through His eyes, we realize that we can now choose through the power of prayer and the perspective of time to accept His Love and so be healed. We grow spiritually and so are healed in our *choice* to accept Jesus rather than continuing to accept the pain of our experience.

Many people mistakenly think that healing of memories means being able to forget the past, to forget all the situations that have caused us pain. If that were the case, however, we would not know who we are, for much of our identity comes from our previous experiences. There are, on the other hand, several religious cults that attempt to "reprogram" initiates by working with them to forget significant parts of their past; what these cults do is an incomplete and dangerous substitute for that which Jesus wants for all of us through healing of memories.

Rather, in healing of memories, what we forget is the *pain;* we remember the incident but the pain has left it, because the "place" inside us where the pain was through prayer now becomes filled with the Love of Jesus. His Love is the creative energy by which we are healed.

How Our Memories Can Be Healed

Healing of memories is based on the fact of Jesus' eternal Love for all human beings. At every stage and in every event of our lives, Jesus has known us and loved us, and it has been His desire to use every minute of our lives to bring us closer to Him. He has walked every step with us, offering to us at each turn of events whatever we needed to live creatively.

If we find this statement difficult to believe, we must ask ourselves what we think love is. Which one of us, if we had a dear friend whom we loved deeply and who was in trouble, would not take the time and effort to help that person if we had the power to do so? None of us, of course! And yet, when we think of God's loving us, we do not see His Love in these practical terms. We make His Love abstract, impersonal, and ethereal, when in fact He is the Author of all that is concrete, personal, and real. The nature of love is active. If our own love will not allow us to sit back passively and see a loved one remain in pain, how much more active is the Love of God, Who has all power to help and all goodness as a motive to act?

Sometimes, then, as we have walked through our lives, we have seen God's Love for us and have accepted it into our inner selves. In these moments we have become strong, creative, loving, free. In these experiences we have grown spiritually. These are the experiences on which we build our futures; these are the experiences we are proud and happy to remember.

At other moments, however, we have rejected His Love— not that we would have done so if we had known exactly what we were doing, but we have rejected it nonetheless. This may have happened for one of many different reasons. It may be that the person who was hurting us was a person on whom we depended to reveal God's Love to us, and so we were confused. It may be that the pain of the situation was so great that we could not even think clearly enough to look for Jesus at our side. It may be that the situation developed too fast for us and we did not have a well-developed habit of turning to Jesus in every situation. It may be that we were too young to know how, on our own, to turn to Jesus for love. It may be that we felt guilty for some sin in our lives and thought—incorrectly, of course— that Jesus would not help us because of our sin. It may be that we had not allowed anyone to help us with anything for a long time, and in our defensive attitude we did not know how to allow Jesus into our inner selves to help us either.

Whatever the reason, the result was the same: We went through the situation alone, unprotected from evil, feeling unloved and weak. The destructive force of the experience overwhelmed us, and, instead of growing through it, we were hurt. Because we did not know to whom to turn, we bore our pain alone, we suffered, and a part of our inner selves was crippled or maybe even destroyed.

There is also something about the loneliness of this kind of pain that readies us to suffer this way again the next time we are threatened, and so when that threat comes we are less likely to turn to Jesus for help. After a while, we not only turn away from Him (consciously or unconsciously, it makes no difference in the result), but we begin to think that He does not want to help, or even that He is unable to help. Maybe we even conclude that He does not exist at all! In a certain sense—from a self-centered point of view—we are correct, for He does not exist *in our small world* if we are not reaching out to Him for His Love and assistance.

We could let this state of affairs be if it were not for the fact that every experience of our past affects us in the present in some way. Positive experiences give us a positive self-image, free us to be creative and to grow, and affirm us in our best and most loving selves, our true selves. Destructive experiences, on the other hand, do the opposite, affirming our false selves and leading us into a world of negativism, crushed dreams, and fewer and fewer possibilities for the future.

When we live with both positive and destructive experiences influencing our lives we live with an inner war that deprives us of much energy for growing and for creative living and keeps us from being the persons God intends us to be. Therefore, we need healing for the painful experiences of our lives so that they can be redeemed, so that our lives may flow with greater energy in one direction—toward God, toward wholeness.

When we present a memory to Jesus asking Him to heal it,

what we are doing is asking Him to show us the *entire* memory, that is, to help us to see everything that happened. Therefore, we not only remember the scene we have stored in our memories; we ask that we become aware of any other details to which we have not attended until now. But most important, we ask Jesus to reveal to us *how He was present in that situation,* to show us what He was trying to do, to show us how He was trying to love us and protect us or to help us to grow. It is Jesus' presence that makes the scene liberating and healing. Without Him there is only death and destruction; with Him there is the Cross and the resurrection, life and growth.

As we see our memory from Jesus' point of view we are able to choose a second time—through the grace that comes to us in prayer—how we shall respond in the situation: Do we choose to continue to face this situation alone and be hurt, or do we choose to accept Jesus' Love and be healed? As we turn to the Lord and accept His Love into our conscious awareness of this memory, He opens to us a new way to resolve the problem.

Sometimes we see Him applying to us the sufferings of His own Passion—taking blows for us, taking insults, taking to Himself the pain of betrayal, suffering our loneliness, fear, grief, confusion, doubt, or physical pain—and turning to us with acceptance and compassion in His eyes. His Love flows into that inner space where we were carrying pain and our true selves are set free.

Sometimes all we need to know is that Jesus was appreciating us and accepting us unconditionally while we were enduring a degrading episode of our lives, or while we ourselves were sinning and turning from Him. Sometimes we need our heavenly Father, Mother, or Brother to take us into His or her arms so that we might be at peace within. Sometimes we need to see another person in a new light and learn to forgive that person to find our inner peace (Chapter 5); in these situations Jesus sometimes first heals the hurt that the other person caused us so that we literally have nothing to hold against that person anymore, and in forgiving the person we let go of our pain and are free to grow because of that experience.

In a sense, then, after we pray for healing of memories we

have "two pasts." While the historical events of our lives have not changed in themselves and so our factual past is still quite real to us, our *perception* of those events has now been expanded to include the presence of Jesus, and He has completely transformed the *meaning* of those events. They are no longer destructive but rather creative. No longer do they end in death; rather, in the power and Love of Jesus they have pierced through death and entered a resurrection glory. And is not the latter our "real past"? For Jesus was indeed with us in each of those events, and healing of memories merely frees us to understand for the first time what was really happening and what was the real significance of this event.

Healing Is Possible for Every Memory

It is obvious to many of us that we need healing for these destructive experiences so that they will not continue to destroy our inner selves. It is not always so obvious that we need healing for every memory, destructive and constructive! Why, we ask, would we need healing for a constructive experience? The answer is simply that without Jesus we cannot fully appreciate that experience, that is, we cannot entirely take it into our inner selves and derive from it the life that God intends for us to have from it.

If we find this statement improbable, maybe we can look again at an example we used in a slightly different context in Chapter 5, that is, the way in which we accept compliments. We noted in Chapter 5 that when many people are complimented they do anything but accept the compliment as true: They change the subject, ignore the statement, immediately return another compliment of a similar nature, explain away that for which they have been complimented, or remain silent. In other words, when faced with a potentially constructive experience, an experience from which we could grow and derive much life, many of us refuse to take it into our inner selves. We refuse to appreciate our experience!

The way in which we handle compliments is a good measuring stick for the way we tend to handle all positive experiences. If we find ourselves not believing or trusting compliments sincerely given, or if we find ourselves rejecting them in any subtle or overt way, we can be sure that we are doing something similar to all our constructive experiences. Somehow we are distancing ourselves from them, and therefore we are not allowing our inner selves to feed on them. We are preventing ourselves from growing.

We can comprehend this analysis of our lives more easily once we realize that it is psychologically impossible to do the one thing that most of us want to do in this area: It is impossible to choose to distance ourselves only from our destructive experiences. If we are in the habit of not realistically handling our destructive experiences—a habit we would need to develop if we could not handle them creatively, and therefore a habit we would need to develop if we do not face them with Jesus—then we will begin to treat our constructive experiences in just the same way, not because it makes sense to do so, but merely because the human psyche cannot act in a selective way. If we decide to cut off one part of life from our experience, slowly but definitely our minds will begin to have the same attitude toward all of life.

Therefore, we can see that we do not choose to ignore our positive experiences, but rather we make a choice not to pay attention to one part of our lives (usually destructive) because we do not know what to do with it, and this choice soon has its effect on the way we experience our entire lives. We can see, then, how important it is to face each moment of our lives with Jesus at our side; for with Him we need not fear being able to handle any experience that may come our way. In the midst of potentially destructive experiences He will show us the way that will help us grow through them; and as we face constructive experiences we will be able to be open to them, because in the presence of Jesus we do not need to build defensive walls around our inner selves.

We can learn, then, to present our constructive experiences to Jesus for healing, too—"healing" in the sense that we want to relive those experiences with Jesus at our side so that this time we can accept and feel fully the good that came to us in them. Consequently, we pray this prayer in the same way in which we would pray to be healed of a destructive memory. We recall the memory detail for detail, but this time seeing things as they really were—with Jesus in the midst of everything. We note what He says and what He does, the new avenues He opens to us, and the deepened sense of well-being we have when He encourages us to drink in every last drop of goodness from this constructive situation. Thus we learn to let Jesus redeem each experience of our lives, living each experience fully and without fear, for Jesus is with us to protect, to encourage, to love, and to heal. Thus every experience we have can contribute to our spiritual growth.

As we learn to pray in this fashion, we become free to live our present-day lives in this way as well. Maybe this is the most important effect of the prayer for the healing of memories. When experienced over a period of months and years, healing of memories often begins to free us from any fear of life we may have, and from the fear of living life fully. Through it we begin to develop a new confidence in ourselves, for in this prayer we are gathering tangible proof that God loves us just as we are and that He walks our lives with us. We are free to express our true selves, and we are freed to be among the builders of the Kingdom of God on earth.

Praying for Healing of Our Memories

In this part of the book we will outline three methods of prayer that can be used to pray for healing of memories. By no means are these all the ways that are possible to pray this kind of prayer; similarly, we will be able only to begin to describe each of these three kinds of prayer. It is my hope that these chapters will serve as a stimulus to read more on the topic and to discover new and unique ways to pray for healing of memories. Also, it is my hope that the sample prayers that conclude each chapter will serve to teach the method of approaching prayer for healing of memories, and that, instead of being constrained to use these prayers word for word, every reader will be freed to pray these and similar prayers in their own words.

The three ways of praying we will investigate are these: seeing Christ in the events of our lives, seeing ourselves in the events of Christ's life, and focusing on a feeling that we do not fully appreciate in our lives.

Study Guide

1. How do you evaluate the idea that we in part choose our illnesses, or that at least we choose our response to what happens to us in life? What feelings does this idea bring up in you?
2. What are your reactions when you hear how it may be possible that your painful memories can be healed? that through healing of memories prayer you could appreciate your constructive memories more fully?
3. When you look inside yourself, do you sense that a war is going on between your positive and destructive experiences trying to influence your present life? Explain. (Answer only after a few minutes of silent reflection.)
4. Describe your feelings during an experience of healing of memories in your own life, or describe how you imagine healing of memories might feel to you.
5. What will be necessary for *you* to accept Jesus' presence into your yet unhealed memories?
6. Which constructive experiences of your life have you been rejecting and therefore are now ones in which you need to see the presence of Jesus through healing prayer?
7. Describe any experiences that lead you to see a correlation between inner healing and physical healing—between inner healing and spiritual growth.

Suggested Reading

Dobson, Theodore E. *Inner Healing: God's Great Assurance.* New York: Paulist Press, 1978.

MacNutt, Francis. *Healing.* Notre Dame, IN: Ave Maria Press, 1974.

———. *The Power to Heal.* Notre Dame, IN: Ave Maria Press, 1978.

Puhl, Louis J., S.J., trans. *The Spiritual Exercises of St. Ignatius.* Chicago: Loyola University Press, 1951.

Shlemon, Barbara Leahy. *Healing the Hidden Self.* Notre Dame, IN: Ave Maria Press, 1981.

Stapleton, Ruth Carter. *The Experience of Inner Healing.* Waco, TX: Word, Inc., 1978.

———. *The Gift of Inner Healing.*

Tapscott, Betty. *Inner Healing through Healing of Memories.* Privately published, 1975.

Chapter 8
Seeing Christ in the Events of Our Lives

Union with Jesus is the first goal of the Christian life. This is the primary way in which a Christian experiences spiritual growth, for it is in Christ that we have been given every spiritual blessing, and it is through Christ that we have been adopted as God's own children (Eph 1:3–5). While God has given to us all that is important, we can make use of His gifts only to the extent to which we are one with Christ, for all of these gifts are given to us "in Him." When we live in Him, we can learn to see, appreciate, understand, and use the gifts God gives to us completely, and thus we are free to grow spiritually.

Therefore, faithful Christians spend much time and energy trying to come close to Christ. We read the Scriptures, we pray alone and in groups, we study, we try to conform our lives to His Gospel, we yield to His Spirit's gifts. When we do all these things simultaneously depending on His grace and love, we are living good Christian lives.

Why, then, do many faithful Christians not find the total freedom and joy that the Gospel promises to one who follows its way? Presuming that these unfulfilled Christians are sincere in their walk with Christ and are not kidding themselves into believing that they are doing more than they really are, there is yet *one more thing* that is required. Sometimes it happens spontaneously to a person as he or she lives the Christian life outlined above; but more often than not, it needs to begin with a definite choice on the part of the Christian who seeks the abundant life that Jesus promises (cf. Jn 10:10). That one thing is inner healing, especially healing of memories.

Why is healing of memories so important? Because our past makes up as much of us as our present does; the Christian life outlined above brings Christ only into our present, and healing of memories brings Christ into our past. Furthermore, we will soon see that the phrases "inner healing" and "healing of memories" are contemporary descriptions of fundamental Gospel truths.

General Principles

Paul understood why we need Christ in our past: "... you must put aside your old self.... Your mind must be renewed by a spiritual revolution so that you can put on the new self that has been created in God's way, in the goodness and holiness of the truth" (Eph 4:22–24). Up to the point in our lives at which we began to take Jesus seriously, our minds were the playgrounds of all kinds of ideas and feelings. Some of them were good, holy, and true, but often not many were. And even after we accepted Jesus personally into our lives as a savior, we have not always accepted His invitation to spiritual growth, but at times we have given over our minds to evil, unholy, and false ways.

Our old selves, the false and confused persons we were in the past, have been formed by these ways and so the work of the Spirit must be enacted in our minds, that is, we need a spiritual revolution in them. Notice that we are not looking for a psychological revolution in our minds—we are not looking for humanly created thoughts and feelings to fill our minds, no matter how new or different they might be. Rather, we look for a *spiritual* revolution in our minds—a way for the Spirit of God to change entirely the ways in which we think, feel, imagine, decide, and remember.

Who or what could take over our minds and entirely revolutionize them? Surely humanistic psychology cannot do it; as powerful and important as it is when it is used properly (in relationship to God), psychology ultimately relies on one set of thoughts and feelings to replace another, and that is not the spiritual revolution and renewal of the person that we seek. Surely religious and/or secular cults cannot do it (anything from the Hare Krishnas to mind control to witchcraft); for they are either an irresponsible variant of humanistic psychology or they put people in touch with a spiritual power that is not good, holy, and true—for not all spirits are good spirits, and not all spirits are looking out for our welfare.

Only Jesus has the power that we seek. Only Jesus can revolutionize our minds "in God's way, in the goodness and holiness of the truth" (Eph 4:24b).

But, typical of Jesus, His form of revolution is both gentle and strong. He does not want to bulldoze His way into our minds, clearing out piles of feelings here and destroying structures built on foundations of false ideas there. His way is far more sensitive than that, far more respectful of the uniqueness and fragility of each human being, far more constructive and far-sighted. His way of revolutionizing our minds is by revolutionizing one by one each event in our memories (as well as all the contents of the other functions of our minds, as we saw in Parts One and Two of this book).

Our memories retain for us our experiences; they are the points of convergence for our thoughts, decisions, and feelings. It is in our memories that many of our present-day feelings have their roots, that many of the thoughts that now rule our minds have their origins, that the decisions of the past continue to live and affect the present. Each of our experiences has been carefully recorded by our brains and is available for replay, consciously or unconsciously, at any time. It is a medical fact established by Dr. Wilder Penfield in his research into the human brain conducted at McGill University in Toronto, Canada, in the 1950s, that our entire past is stored within us and greatly affects our present-day lives, whether we want it to or not.

All we need to do, then, to understand our need to allow Christ to enter every event of our lives is to remember some of the times in which we have been hurt, confused, mistreated, overdisciplined, underdisciplined, maligned, physically abused, unloved, ignored, or the victim of other people's sins. Similarly, we can also remember some of the times we have sinned against others and stop to see how those sins distorted our personalities, our expectations of ourselves, and our ability to live in the freedom of the children of God. When we stop to realize that all these experiences are still alive within us and continuing to do damage to our inner selves, we realize that we need salvation in each of our memories if we are to grow spiritually to reach the destiny God has planned for us as His children.

Ever since each of us first heard the Christian message, we have heard that we must give ourselves to Christ to find our salvation. Seeing Christ in the events of our lives is precisely a way of doing that. It is not a new message, for this message of inner renewal, the spiritual revolution of our minds, is part of the fabric of the New Testament, and is even prefigured in the Old Testament (e.g., in Is 53:4–5 and Ps 30:2). Phrases like "inner healing" and "healing of memories" are new, but they are merely an attempt to help contemporary minds understand a scriptural and traditional teaching that says that Jesus has the power and the Love to renew every part of us, inside and out.

The genius of healing of memories, however, is that it is a way of praying that allows God to accomplish this task step by step, memory by memory; it is therefore a way of praying that allows us to know His Love concretely, not abstractly. In praying about each memory, we are allowing Jesus to "plant" Himself in various events all through our lives.

Often Jesus used the imagery of planting, caring for, and harvesting a field of grain or a vineyard to explain the movement of the Kingdom of God within each human being, and what is the Kingdom of God within us if it is not the presence of Jesus? As we present each memory to Jesus for Him to heal, He reveals His presence in that memory, thus planting Himself there. As His presence grows and matures in these memories, we grow and mature in Christ.

Another aspect of planting that is applicable to the way Jesus grows within us is the way some plants, for example bulb plants, divide and spread on their own. One year we may plant tulip bulbs one foot apart from each other, but after three or four years we will have a full bed of tulips because tulip bulbs multiply and spread underground every year. Similarly, as we "plant" Jesus in various times of our lives—for example, in one memory from the age of three, another from the age of ten, another from our teen-age years, and so on—He spreads His presence and His influence finally to encompass our entire lives. This is one of the meanings of the Parables of Great Assurance (Mt 13:31–33), so called because they assure us of God's continuing presence in our lives.

In accomplishing this revolution memory by memory, Jesus gives us a kind of growth that is slow and therefore one to which we can adjust with relative ease. He also gives us reason to trust His Love, for trust is something that also grows slowly. Further, He establishes us as builders of His Kingdom; for His goal is not merely the healing of a memory and the freedom from pain and limitation that results from such a healing—although our happiness and freedom are important to Him; rather, His goal is the healing of our entire lives and saving us, bringing us out of the dark realms of destruction and making of us a creative force that has the power and authority to build the Kingdom of God on earth.

Finally, as we pray to see Christ in the events of our lives, we need to remember a point first explained in the Introduction to Part III, namely, that when we pray any kind of prayer for healing of memories, we are not "bringing Christ into the situation"; rather, we are asking Him to reveal the ways in which He *already has been present* in the situation, and we are further asking Him to give us the strength to choose to accept His presence there as more important than the pain we felt. To view healing of memories in any other way is to make magic of it, that is, telling God to go here and there within our memories and do what we want Him to do in them, creating for us a past that, in a certain sense, could merely be a product of our own minds.

No, the beauty of healing of memories is that we are not inventing anything with our imagination; rather, our imaginations under the direction of the Holy Spirit are revealing to us the truth we have not seen all along, that is, the fact that Jesus appreciated and accepted us completely even when we were in the midst of the most destructive, the most abhorrent, and the most sinful situations. We did not see or accept His Love in these situations, and that is the reason we were hurt. In accepting Jesus' Love we are healed.

A Description of the Prayer

The first step in learning to pray healing of memories by seeing Christ in the events of our lives is to identify a memory that Jesus wants to heal now. Again, as in many of the previous chapters of this book, we begin by seeking the Spirit's guidance, for doing so makes the difference between using a mental technology and praying. If we were to select on our own the memory we wanted Jesus to heal, we would be in control of the situation, and whoever is in control is master. Since all healing prayer is aimed at allowing Jesus to more and more become our Lord and Master, we seek His Spirit to unveil the memory for which we need to pray.

To do this is not a difficult or complicated task. We begin with prayer, asking God to stir His Spirit and reveal what He wants healed in this time and place. We know He will answer this prayer because we asked Him to (cf. Lk 11:9–13). We may find that writing our thoughts in a journal (Chapter 3) will help us to concretize our perceptions and reveal to us the roots of the patterns in our lives that need healing. But whether or not we write, we consider our lives by looking with Jesus to find the source of our pain.

So, after we pray for guidance, we begin with the situation in our present life in which the Spirit has revealed that we need healing, and we see if there are any memories that are the roots of this situation. On the other hand, there are times we do not come to the Lord with a focused awareness of a particular situation in our daily lives. Then we can review in a prayerful way the persons, places, and events of our personal histories, asking the Lord to let us know where He wants us to stop and pray for healing. He may bring to our attention a destructive memory or a constructive one, as we saw in the Introduction to Part Three.

If we allow the Holy Spirit to be in charge of the process by which memories are released from our unconscious minds into our consciousness, we will never be confronted with a memory too powerful for us to handle. In His widsom, the Spirit reveals only memories with which we can cope, and He will slowly strengthen us to be able to handle the deeper and often more important memories at some future time. If, on the other hand, we were to probe into our minds on our own powers, through introspection and guided by our own desires, we could uncover all kinds of material we could not handle. It has been a sobering experience for me to meet many people who have been harmed, some of them seriously, by probing into their own minds without Jesus' Light to guide them. But when we have prayed for guidance, we know that He will take care of us by giving us guidance, because we trust Him to be faithful to His Word and we trust Him to love us.

After we have identified the area in which the Lord wants to work at this time, we ready ourselves for the prayer for healing of memories. We center ourselves using the steps mentioned in the last section of the Preface, and we begin to pray by thanking God for the person for whom we are praying, even and especially if that person is oneself. For if we do not feel accepted and loved by God, it will be more than difficult to accept the gift of His healing when He gives it.

Next, we describe in loving detail the scene for which we need healing. We remember what happened, we remember how we felt. We describe not only what happened as our factual memories recall it, but we also ask Jesus to show us how He was acting in that situation. We notice how He ministers to all the people in the scene: We notice what He says and what He does; we follow His lead as He asks us to forgive another or to understand another from that person's point of view, and/or to

have compassion on ourselves in that situation; we accept into
the depth of our own hearts the Love He has for us in the midst
of all the pain we recall; and we see Him befriending us in just
the way we need to be befriended, meeting our deepest needs.

We remember, however, that as we pray we do not invent
all these things in our own imaginations; rather, because we
have asked the Holy Spirit to guide us, we allow our intuitions
to apprehend what Jesus actually was doing for us in that event
long ago. Thus, this kind of prayer puts us in touch with
Reality, not illusion, and we are seeing this event in its completeness (i.e., including Jesus) for the first time.

If we have trouble imagining how Jesus was loving us in
the situation, that is, if our spiritual intuitions are inhibited
because of unfamiliarity with the prayer or because of some
block in our personal relationship with Jesus (for example, guilt
over a sin we have committed), we can use as our guide stories
from the Gospels, seeing in them how Jesus treated people in
need. If Jesus treated people a certain way then, He treats us in
just the same way now, for "Jesus Christ is the same today as he
was yesterday and as he will be forever" (Heb 13:8). If Jesus
healed the sick then, He heals us who are sick now. If He
forgave sins then, He forgives us in our sinfulness now. If He
freed people from shame, indignity, and aimless living then, He
does the same for us now.

As we see what Jesus was doing for us, even though at the
time it occurred in history we did not understand what He was
doing and maybe did not even care, it is important that we
consciously choose to accept His Love into our hearts. While some
people can make too much of this point, others can make too
little of it.

Choosing to accept Jesus' Love for us in prayer for the
healing of memories makes the difference between merely experiencing a temporary emotional "high" on the one hand and
beginning to live a spiritually new and freer kind of life on the
other. The first makes us feel good for the moment but has no
lasting effect; the second is the beginning of a new stage in
living a Jesus-centered, creative wholeness. Maybe it is this

implicit responsibility to live in a different way that makes some people avoid this subtle but crucial step, but this is the step that frees us to grow spiritually through healing of memories prayer.

As we choose to accept Jesus' Love for us, we are also choosing to accept this experience and to cherish it as our own. If we are dealing with a destructive situation, in the past we have disowned it because of the pain in it; because we have not seen its value and worth, we have tried to forget the memory by repressing it into our unconscious minds. Through the prayer to see Christ in this event, the pain of the event is healed by Jesus' Love for us and we come to see the good that is there for us in the situation, namely, that this situation now has become an occasion to which we can point saying, "See, here is another time in which Jesus proved He loves me!" This is what Dennis and Matthew Linn call "seeing the gift in the pain."

Through the prayer for healing of memories, then, we can begin to reclaim moments of our lives that we had previously thrown away as if they were garbage, and thus we become more of who we truly are and who we were meant to be when God created us (our true selves). As we come to see this kind of giftedness in our own lives, whatever we may have been in the past, we have more vitality in our living as well as more to share with others in ministry and service. We become a healing personality for others, "wounded healers" as Henri Nouwen phrases it, through this spiritual growth.

Finally, we conclude the prayer with a word of thanksgiving and a request for peace. We thank God for all that He has done in the prayer and all that He will continue to do within us after we have stopped praying. This last is not an unimportant point, for it again marks one of the major differences between psychological healing and divine healing through healing of memories: The power of healing through prayer remains just as strong within the person for whom the prayer has been prayed and even grows stronger after the prayer is over, because that power is a Divine Person Who has been given more freedom to live within because of the prayer. Finally, we pray for peace so that no alien force, whether earthly or demonic, will disturb what has begun in the healing prayer.

An Example

During the summer of 1979 I had begun to discover that, while I had many fine relationships and even close friendships with several women, I expressed in many little ways in my thoughts, words, and deeds an antipathy for feminine thinking and feminine behavior. In trying to look at my feelings more closely, I realized that they had to do with the fact that I am adopted, and with the woman who had given me life and then given me away before I could ever know her, my natural mother. When I thought about her I realized that I had few if any conscious feelings for her: I had some attitudes about her—good, indifferent, and bad—but no feelings like love, concern, or even hate. I felt nothing for her.

It was when I was ready to deal with the problem that I found the right person (and the right time, place, and circumstances) with whom to pray. As this person began to pray with me, I went back in my memory to the home of my childhood. Jesus was with me at age three or four in that backyard so familiar to me, and I was angry. No, I was enraged. As the person praying with me recalled to my mind the mother who gave me birth, I saw myself venting years of pent-up anger on Jesus; I beat my little fists on His thigh, I ran around the garden and pulled up all the flowers (I have always loved flowers). I saw myself running into the house and destroying the living room, knocking over tables and lamps. I unleashed a temper tantrum in my imagination the likes of which I had never enacted in reality. The anger that I had held within me at this woman who had given me away finally was out in the open and expressed. And through it all, Jesus loved me and understood.

When I finally had finished my rampage and Jesus' Love had saturated me, He gently but firmly took me by the shoulders and said, "Now can we talk?" At this time the person who was praying with me asked me what was going on and I told her all that had happened. She told me to ask Jesus what He wanted me to do next. He suggested that I look at my mother in a new way. With the sensitive help of my partner in prayer, I saw my mother in my imagination while she was pregnant with me, and

I listened to her pray to Jesus and to Mary, asking them to help her to be a good mother. I suffered with her in her decision to give me up for adoption. Then, as an adult, I sat across from her and talked with her; we shared our feelings about each other—our mutual sorrow for our situation, and our mutual love and pride in each other—and for the first time I was able to see her as a person, say good-bye to her, and grieve the loss of her.

During the prayer I could see that she was and is a good mother, and I felt her love and her strength coming into me. I began the prayer by hating her because she gave me away, but by the end of the prayer I saw that I loved her dearly. I chose to experience those feelings, and I regretted having to be separated from her. But as I let her go, I realized that she was leaving me in order to be with me in a different way—in the feminine side of my own personality, and in the women who are mother and sister and friend to me in my life now.

After praying this prayer I noticed in my life a new comfortableness with women, a new openness to the feminine aspects of life, and a new ability to live in community relationships (relationships depend on what are traditionally termed as "feminine" virtues such as person-centeredness, earthiness as opposed to stuffiness, and attention to feelings). I had accepted, through forgiveness and healing of memories, the first woman I had known in life, and so had opened myself to all persons and aspects of life that are feminine. The prayer has had a deep effect not only on my own life but also on the lives of the people whom my life touches.

A Sample Prayer

There are many general prayers for healing of memories by seeing Christ in the events of our lives that are available today, including one in the last chapter of my book *Inner Healing: God's Great Assurance.* Many of these prayers take a person on a more-or-less complete journey through life, helping readers to see how Jesus was present in many specific situations with them.

These prayers cover events like the moment of birth; significant or difficult moments with parents, siblings, teachers, and friends; growing into adolescence; relationships with the Church and her representatives; significant sinful moments; and adult relationships up to the present. These kinds of written, general prayers can be important, not only as tools for prayer but also as teachers of how to compose prayers in our own words that meet the more specific needs of our lives.

However, the prayer we will pray now will not be like any of those prayers in several ways: It will not deal with any specific moment in our lives; it will assist us in looking at only a few memories in one area of our lives, which we and the Holy Spirit will choose as the subject matter of the prayer; it will provide us with a general outline with which we will be able to compose, on our own, almost any prayer we want to pray to see Christ in an event of our lives; and we will be able to use it to discover Christ in both our constructive and destructive experiences for our spiritual growth.

Before we pray this prayer, we need to understand, then, that it will ask us to do a little more on our own than most other general prayers for healing of memories that we may have used in the past. As we begin this prayer, let us use the four steps that prepare us to pray, which were outlined in the section of the Preface entitled "A Note on Using the Sample Prayers in This Book." When we have completed them we can begin this prayer.

> *"Thank You, Jesus, for this opportunity to pray to You. I ask You to reveal Yourself in the midst of the events of my life. How assuring it is to know that You are always with me, even though I do not always feel Your presence; how good it is that through prayer You give me a second chance to see You and accept Your Love for me in moments of my life that I have already lived! I appreciate this opportunity to grow, Lord, and I will not use it lightly.*
>
> *"Jesus, please stir Your Holy Spirit within me to*

guide me in this prayer. I come into this moment open
to whatever guidance He may give to me about the area
of my life that He wants to heal now.

"Spirit of God, please reveal to me in a concrete
way the direction You want this prayer to take. Please
give to me all the guidance, all the gifts, and all the
wisdom I will need to pray the perfect prayer You
want prayed for me today. . . ."

Now we spend some time in silence, waiting for the Spirit
to bring into our consciousness the area of our lives that He
wants to be the subject matter of our prayer. It could be a
constructive event or a destructive event in our lives. It could be
from many years ago or from yesterday. We trust that in whatever way He decides to heal us, it will be the best possible
experience we can have at this moment in our lives. When He
brings an issue or event into our minds, we continue.

"Thank You, Lord, for showing me Your will for my
healing at this moment in my life. Thank You, also, for
giving me life so that I can be in touch with You. I
think of the complexity of my body, and I thank
You. . . . I think of all the ways I can experience life,
and I thank You. . . . I think of all the moments of my
life and of the many different facets of my personality,
and I thank You. . . .

"Lord Jesus, let us look at this scene together, this
scene that Your Spirit has brought to my mind for
healing. Help me to remember every detail of what
happened and how I felt about what happened. But do
not let me remember only that: Help me to see how
You were in that situation with me, what You were
saying, what You were doing, how You were minister-
ing to all of the people involved in this event. . . . Jesus,
I look at You and I am attracted by Your Love, Your
gentleness, Your strength. You know just what to do to
make this situation the best it can be. Give me the grace
to turn to You and to choose to accept Your Love for

*me into my heart in whatever way You choose to show
Your Love. And if You see that I need to forgive
someone or to be forgiven of some sinful aspect of my
life, help me to choose to do that, too."*

Now we remain in silence and let all that we have just read
actually happen in our imaginations. We remain silent for however long it will take to let Jesus deeply into our hearts, accepting us completely, cherishing us, affirming us. We continue to
trust that what we are imagining is actually happening because
we have given the Holy Spirit control of our imaginations. If we
have trouble imagining how Jesus is dealing with our situation,
maybe we can think of a passage in the Gospels in which Jesus
dealt with a problem similar to ours, and in reading it we can
see how He is meeting our needs now. When we sense that this
part of the prayer is over, we can conclude the prayer.

*"Thank You, Jesus, for revealing Yourself within my
own experience. Help me to understand what this
means—that You love me enough to share with me all
the experiences of my life so that I can grow through
them. Thank You for the gift of Your Love. Thank You
for reclaiming this moment of my life for me. Thank
You for giving me yet another reason to love You.
Enfold me now with Your Spirit of peace, so that what
You have begun may not be disturbed by any force in
the universe. When the power of Your healing Love
has grown strong in me, I promise to use it to serve
others more freely and with greater love, just as You
have served me. Amen."*

Study Guide

1. How have you tried to come close to Christ during your life?
   In what ways have you been successful, and in what ways
   have you been unsuccessful? What are your feelings about
   your success and failure in your search for spiritual growth?

2. Do you think that secular and spiritual cults lead people down a blind alley? What has been your experience with them?
3. What does healing of memories offer to you that is different from other spiritualities or ways of praying that you have used in the past?
4. What do you think it will do for you to see Christ in each of the memories of your life?
5. What are some of the dangers that you see in praying for healing of memories but not requesting or accepting the guidance of the Holy Spirit?
6. How do you think seeing Jesus present in every detail of a memory will change your perception of that memory?

Suggested Reading

Dobson, Theodore E. *Inner Healing: God's Great Assurance.* New York: Paulist Press, 1978.

Sanford, Agnes. *The Healing Light.* Plainfield, NJ: Logos International, 1978.

Shlemon, Barbara Leahy. *Healing the Hidden Self.* Notre Dame, IN: Ave Maria Press, 1981.

Stapleton, Ruth Carter. *The Experience of Inner Healing.* Waco, TX: Word, Inc., 1978.

————. *The Gift of Inner Healing.*

Tapscott, Betty. *Inner Healing through Healing of Memories.* Privately published, 1975.

Chapter 9
Seeing Ourselves in the Events of Christ's Life

Healing of memories is a way of uniting our memories with Christ. It is a way of acknowledging and accepting His presence in our lives, soaking in His Love, and acting on His challenge to live as loved people rather than as desolate people (cf. Hos 2:24). To grow spiritually through prayer for healing of memories, then, we need to touch the real Jesus, Who lives both outside of us and within us.

In the last chapter we investigated a way to contact Jesus as He lives within our inner selves. In this chapter we will look at a way to contact Jesus as He lives outside of us, especially in Scripture, and see how He can touch our memories and free our past as we unite ourselves with the events of His own life.

It is important to learn to pray seeing ourselves in the events of Christ's life as a balance to praying to see Christ in the events of our lives. For that kind of praying can subtly become self-centered or can reinforce our self-centered tendencies. When we seek only to see Christ in our own lives we can unconsciously encourage the erroneous notion that we are the center of the universe, and that even God centers Himself on us. This is not the message that healing of memories prayer ought to convey, and it does not convey this message to one who understands and prays for it properly. But, unfortunately, we do not always do things properly.

While Jesus wants us to know that we are very important to

Him, we also need to know that He is the center of the universe, not we. As we come to understand this truth we can live creative, whole, and wholesome lives because we are in proper relationship to the real order of things. Praying to see ourselves in the events of Christ's life conveys to us more graphically than any other kind of inner healing prayer how much we need Jesus to grow spiritually, and how much God is in control of our entire lives and especially of the growth process.

General Principles

Seeing ourselves in the events of Christ's life is a way of praying for healing of memories that will be familiar to anyone who is aware of the *Spiritual Exercises* of St. Ignatius of Loyola. It is a kind of scriptural meditation in which the words of Scripture and our imaginations interplay with each other. Thus, it is a way of making the Scriptures come alive.

We find a scriptural basis for this kind of prayer in these words of Jesus: "On that day you will understand that I am in my Father and you in me and I in you" (Jn 14:20). In this one sentence Jesus reveals an entire world view; in these words He explains how He sees the world operating.

"On that day" is a phrase used by the prophets for occasions when God dramatically shows Himself in history. A "day" in this sense would be more accurately described as an event or an epoch. Often the prophets used this phrase to refer to a special epoch, the age of the Messiah, the time when the Messiah would be revealed. Of course, we know that time is now, and the way that the Messiah has been revealed is that He has risen from the dead. So we can insert this idea in the sentence to understand better the meaning of Jesus' words: When I rise from the dead you will understand that I am in my Father and you are in me and I am in you.

It is because the Father raised Jesus from the dead that we understand that He and the Father are one; it is because He is risen that we understand that He is in us and we in Him. Healing of memories works, we can see, because Jesus died and rose from the dead; it does not work because we want it to, because we say the right words, or because we use our imaginations and so make this prayer feel more lively than other prayers. Because Jesus rose from the dead, He can live in us (seeing Christ in the events of our lives) and we can live in Him (seeing ourselves in the events of Christ's life). These ways of praying for healing of memories, in other words, fulfill the Scriptures and help every part of us—our past as well as our present and our future—to be one with Him.

Another benefit of praying to see ourselves in the events of Christ's life is that by doing so we can come to discover from the inside the power that made Jesus' life great. By placing ourselves in a close and personal relationship with Him and seeing ourselves as persons whom He heals or with whom He converses, or by so closely identifying with Him that, because He lives in us and we in Him, we take His place in a scene from His own personal life, for example, His birth or His baptism, we can begin to have an inside view of how and why He did the things He did. By entering the life of Christ in this way we come to an understanding of Him that our intellects alone cannot give because, for a while, through our imaginations we walk in His sandals, we feel His healing touch, or we hear His captivating words.

In an age when we want so much to rediscover the power of the Bible to heal, to console, and to help us grow spiritually, this kind of inner healing prayer is more than appropriate. Sometimes when we read the Bible we forget that "the word of God is something alive and active" (Heb 4:12), and in forgetting that truth we read the Bible as if it were another book. Thus we are not open to its unique power to transform our lives and therefore we are not transformed by it and we do not grow spiritually when we read it. Praying to see ourselves in the events of Christ's life is a simple and straightforward way to allow the Scriptures to be alive to us, to be a living word that we allow to change the way we live.

Also, when we put ourselves into the Scripture in this personal way, thus meeting Christ, we find that "no created thing can hide from Him; everything is uncovered and open to the eyes of the One to whom we must give an account of ourselves" (Heb 4:13). If, as we saw in the last chapter using the words of Paul, we are to "put on the new self that has been created in God's way, in the goodness and holiness of the *truth*" (Eph 4:24, emphasis mine), then we need to come to the Scriptures, where the truth of our lives in Christ will be uncovered and revealed. This process is at the center of spiritual growth, inner healing, and healing of memories, and the Scripture is an important part of this aspect of healing.

Some of us may say, however, that we cannot identify in such an intimate way with Christ because He was and is so perfect and sinless, and our sinful lives have little to do with His life. While it is true that "He is without sin" (Heb 4:15b), it is also true that He "has been tempted in every way that we are" (Heb 4:15a), that He suffered much and "offered up prayer and entreaty, aloud and in silent tears" (Heb 5:7a), and that "He submitted so humbly ... (and) learned to obey through suffering" (Heb 5:7b). Surely, while He is fully and completely God, He is also fully and completely human, and so understands far better than we would like to admit what it means to be tempted, under trial, disappointed, lonely, hurt, upset, angry, and betrayed. "For it is not as if we had a high priest who was incapable of feeling our weaknesses with us" (Heb 4:15a); no, Jesus understands all too well the limitations and pain of human existence—both His and ours. If we want to see a life in which more human suffering occurred than in any other, all we need to do is read the Gospels. Anyway, is not our sin often our way to attempt to avoid the suffering to which the process of spiritual growth calls us?

Jesus understands our weakness for He has experienced temptations to moral weakness in His own life; He also found Himself physically helpless, especially during His Passion. And He has lived through our weakness with us. As we approach Him through the Scriptures we have no need to fear Him (unless we are afraid of the truth) nor can we prejudge Him to be insensitive to our lives (unless we want to say that the Scriptures lie, that He is not a full human being, and that He does not love us). Praying to see ourselves in the events of

Christ's life is a way to come to know the truth of Jesus, to Whom we want to draw close, so that we can live in the way that He did, that is, by His commandments, and in so doing know the truth that will set us free (Jn 8:31–32).

A Description of the Prayer

We begin our prayer to see ourselves in the events of Christ's life in the same way we begin any prayer for healing of memories—by asking the Lord's guidance to help us identify a memory that He wants to heal now. Therefore, we pray for guidance, we talk with a friend, we journalize, we review our lives—all the things we reviewed under this point as we investigated it in the last chapter. Most important, we are constantly asking the Holy Spirit to be in charge of the process by which memories are released from our unconscious minds into our consciousness. By allowing the Spirit to be in charge in this way we are assured that He is the origin of the healing we will experience, and we will also be protected from the bumbling ways that we or others have of probing into our minds on our own looking for areas that need healing.

Next, we ask the Lord to show us when He faced a similar situation in His own life, either in an event He lived or in a story He told. If at this point we remain silent for awhile and wait for Jesus to answer our prayer, we will often be surprised how a story from Scripture will suddenly come into our minds or we will open our Bible to a story that will help us to pray. If we are seeking healing for a destructive memory in our lives and we cannot immediately identify with a story from any other part of Jesus' life, usually in the accounts of His Passion and Death we will find a scene in which we can identify with His pain and weakness.

As we find a scene from Christ's life that relates to our need, we may want to look it up in the Gospels to help us to be accurate in our account of the details. Often when we do this, we are surprised by one or another detail that we had forgotten, but that has special poignancy in our situation. Also, as we use the Scriptures themselves and not merely our memory of the Scriptures, we bring into our prayer a heightened sense of the life-giving power of the Word of God.

When we have the story before us, we need to find a way to be able to use the wealth of wisdom and love in it. A simple way to accomplish this goal is to divide the story into beginning, middle, and end. As we continue in prayer using this story, then, we use one section at a time, allowing the full impact of it to affect us. When we use sections of the story one at a time instead of the entire story all at once, we are not overwhelmed with all the details, nuances, and dialogue among the persons in the story. Using one section at a time gives us something we can more easily grasp, appreciate, and interiorize.

As we read each section of the story we become a part of it. We enter the story as a bystander or as an eyewitness watching the story unfold in our own experience; or we enter it in the place of the person to whom Jesus spoke or ministered, thus allowing ourselves to be the personal recipients of the love, the care, the discipline, the healing that He gave to the person in the actual story; or we enter it in the person of Jesus Himself—remembering Jesus' words: "You [are] in me and I in you" (Jn 14:20b)—to experience, for example, a healing of our births in His birth, or a healing of our betrayal in His betrayal, and so forth.

After we choose a way to enter the story, we read the verses from the passage quietly and meditatively, but we also read "in between the lines." We imagine the words that were said but not recorded, the gestures, tones of voice, and nuances of relationship of which there are only hints in the text, and the sights, sounds, smells, and feelings that the people involved in the story experienced. Through our imaginations, under the guidance of the Holy Spirit, we make all these details our own, we experience them as our own experience.

Thus, we allow this event to have the same impact on us as it would if we were to have lived through it in our own personal history. In allowing the experience to be our own, we also accept the consequence of this experience in the lives of those who did live it—transcendence, strength, hope, healing, spiritual growth. We become so one with Jesus' story that His life flows into us in just the same way it flowed into the people whose personal histories were intertwined with His in Palestine. As we allow ourselves to find our identity in Jesus, the smallness, pettiness, weakness, and sickness of our lives gives way to His great vision, openness, strength, and health. Thus Jesus empowers us to take another step in our spiritual growth.

An Example

All throughout our lives we come in touch more and more with various parts of our personalities, such as our masculinity and femininity, our being sons and daughters of our earthly parents as well as of God our Father and Mary our Mother, our sexual identities, and the roles we play in the lives of others such as mothering and fathering, brothering and sistering, being mothered and fathered, brothered and sistered, befriending and being befriended by others in our lives. As I have walked this journey to become alive to all the relationships that have been given to me, I have found several significant moments of healing and release of my potential to live fully and feel free in those relationships, both spiritual and psychological, with God and with human beings.

One of those significant moments came at a time in which I was seeking a deeper awareness of my sonship to both sets of my earthly parents (natural and adopted) as well as to God. I had the intuition that if I could emotionally experience the fact that I belong to God and am a member of His intimate family circle, I would find released a greater strength in my personhood.

As I was searching for this kind of healing in my life, I happened to find myself in a group in which a prayer to see ourselves in the events of Christ's life was being prayed. While many events in His Life were presented to us, it was the first of them that made the deepest impression on me, for it was the prayer I needed the most.

Reverend Jim Wheeler, S.J., the prayer leader, recreated for us the scene of Bethlehem. As we entered the scene we felt the cold night air, we smelled the wet hay on the ground, we heard the animals in the stable lowing in the background, we felt the excitement of angels in the air. We entered the stable and saw Jesus in the manger, Mary and Joseph sharing their love for each other and for the Child, both tired and yet hopeful, and we felt the presence of Abba watching over them all. Then, because we live in Jesus and He lives in us, we were invited to see ourselves as the baby in the manger, as Abba, Mary, and Joseph completely accepted and appreciated us. We were encouraged to take to ourselves the feelings of pride and joy that those who were there felt for Jesus—to feel them as if they were meant for us, because in a sense they were, for we live in Jesus and He in us.

As we prayed quietly, Father Wheeler helped us to see Joseph pick us up in his hands and hold us over his head in a gesture of fatherly pride; we laughed at the joy of it, but when we again looked into his face, the face was that of our own father and he was playing with us. And when we looked again it was Abba who held us and called us His own with that distinct air of fatherly pride.

I found a new relationship with Abba in that moment of prayer, a new intimacy. The simplicity and creativity of the prayer allowed Abba's love more deeply in my heart than it ever had come before. With that deeper bonding of our relationship I found much healing happening in my self-concept as a person, as a son, and as one who fathers and brothers others. The strength of my inner self began to come forth from me more naturally, not having to be forced. I found a deep and secure identity in being a child of God, and it overflowed into my relationship with my parents. I also found that as I allowed God to be my parent I was learning how to be a spiritual parent to others, to love them into maturity and freedom, to give my life to them especially in my work of spiritual direction. Thus I found renewed meaning in my own life and a deeper sense of the importance of what I do, that is, a sense of mission. I also found myself better able to accept the limitations of my strength and my potential because I knew I was loved for the person I was created to be, not the person I thought I ought to be or the person I wanted to be.

This is the deepest meaning of healing—to accept life, not in the sense of "this is all there is," but in the sense of "there is so much possibility in who I am that I will never find all of it, yet when I find a limitation I know I am not wrong or bad, only human." This is what happens in our inner selves when we let God heal us by bringing us into the events of Jesus' life, and it is an important phase of spiritual growth in the normal Christian life.

A Sample Prayer

There are as many different ways to pray this prayer as there are personal situations to be healed and Gospel stories through which they can be healed. This kind of prayer, as was true for the prayer we learned in the last chapter, can be prayed for constructive or destructive experiences.

The prayer we shall pray here is for experiences in which we have known pain. We shall focus on a time in Christ's life in which many of us can find Him suffering our sorrows and pains, His Passion and Death. If we want to pray a prayer more detailed than the one here, we can use a Gospel text of the Passion and, instead of dividing it up into only three parts, we can use each paragraph or half a paragraph as a section on which to meditate, until we find our way through the entire story.

We prepare ourselves, then, for this prayer by using the four steps mentioned in the section of the Preface entitled "A Note on Using the Sample Prayers in This Book." When we have completed these preparations, we can begin to pray.

"Jesus, I come before You in wonder and awe that You would share Your life so intimately with me. I marvel at how vulnerable You are to me, allowing me into Your very mind and heart. Hold me close, Jesus, and teach me Your ways; show me how to live in the way

You live, and help me to want to grow spiritually through this prayer.

"Spirit of God, move within me and stir those memories of pain, betrayal, hopelessness, and unforgiveness that You want healed in me now. Give me Your strength to allow these memories to come forth so that the grace of this moment will not pass me by, but rather will affect my life forever. . . ."

We now spend some time in silence, waiting for the Spirit to reveal to us the memories that will be our focus for this prayer. We trust Him to bring forth the memories best dealt with at this moment in time. When we have to some extent identified the subject for our prayer, we continue.

"Jesus, let me be with You in Gethsemane, let me feel the cool night air and smell the freshness of spring. You ask Your disciples to pray as You go by Yourself to plead with the Father that what You see must happen will in fact not happen; yet You submit Yourself to His will. Lord, because I live in You and You live in me, let me be in You as You pray. Heal within me the times that I have rebelliously resisted reality, the times I have refused to face my life as it is. . . . Heal my heart of all the times I have said to our Father, 'Not Your will be done, but mine.' . . . Heal me of the fear I have of God's will; as I sense that I am surrounded and filled with You, let Your Love cast out that fear. Bring to my mind any moments in which good could not happen because I was afraid to know, let alone to do God's will; and allow those memories to be engulfed in the power of Your prayer of submission. . . .

"Jesus, let me stay with You as You come back to Your disciples only to find them asleep. How often I, too, have been keenly disappointed by my friends, left alone by them when I needed them the most. Bring to my mind any such moment in my life now; and as You

face Your disciples with love, without condemnation, never attempting to make them feel guilty, heal the pain in my heart over the way I was abandoned by my friends. . . . Forgive me for condemning them, judging them, being bitter toward them. . . . Heal any broken relationships that came from those disappointments, and show me what I must do to repair them. . . .

"Jesus, both You and I have not only been abandoned by friends, but we have also been betrayed. Lord, You know that awful feeling in the pit of Your stomach when You see Your good friend lead the band against You. You know that ever-sinking feeling that comes when the love You have given bears no fruit and all seems wasted. Because I live in You and You live in me, Jesus, let the love You continued to have for Judas flow through me now to my betrayer as well. . . . Help me to forgive that person with the simplicity of Your heart. . . . Help me to pray for that person to be blessed and happy now, coming to know Your Love ever more deeply. . . . Heal the wound that person left in my heart. . . . Teach me how to trust again. . . .

"Jesus, I want to remain one with You as You go before Your accusers to stand trial. How often I have felt on trial in front of my superiors, and even in front of my peers: times I have been called a liar, times no one has believed me, times I was ostracized for my opinions, times I have been corrected in a crude or unjust fashion. Jesus, I need Your patient Love before Your accusers. As You stand there and as I remain within You, let those memories of injustice that You want to heal come into my mind, and as You love Your accusers, let Your Love flow to mine as well. . . . You stood before those men securely because You know Who You are, You know Your identity in the Father. Strengthen my identity in You. Let Your strength come into me so that the words of my accusers do not destroy me. . . . Heal the wounds those situations have

*left in me. . . . Comfort that part of me that is still
shaking with fear and anger and help me to release my
feelings into You now. . . .*

*"Jesus, as difficult as it is, I want to stay in You as
You suffer physically in being beaten, scourged,
crowned with thorns, and in carrying Your Cross. You
suffered the pain of my body then. You bore with
courage many times the pain I have not been able to
bear with complaints. Lord, heal in me the fear of
physical pain . . . the memories of those hospital stays
. . . the many hours of worrying about what the doctors
will find wrong with my body. . . . Jesus, as I walk
through this situation with You, let Your Love heal the
pain of any memories that now come forth. . . .*

*"Jesus, You are crucified. One by one, You relin-
quish every person and thing that means anything to
You—Your mother, Your friends, Your dignity, even
Your right to be angry. And when You are stripped
bare, even Your Father seems to have been taken away:
'My God, My God, why have You abandoned me?'
Jesus, I, too, at times have felt stripped of everything
that is important and have cried out to a God that did
not seem to listen. How I need healing for the pain of
those moments! Jesus, as You give the last energies of
Your life, thank You for letting them flow into me as
strength in these memories of utter distress and failure. . . . Let Your faithfulness now bind my wounds
with peace. . . . Touch that part of my heart that died in
that moment so that it may live again. . . . Touch those
feelings that I promised I would never feel again and
fill them with Your resurrection life. . . . Help me to be
fully myself as I unite myself fully with You. . . .*

*"Lord, I pray for peace. Surround those tender
parts of my mind and my spirit—those parts of me that
You have healed—with a gentleness that will keep
them safe until they are strong. Thank You for all You
have accomplished in me. Help me to remain open to
the consequences of this prayer—the path of spiritual*

growth on which You will be leading me day by day.
Thank You, Jesus, for letting me be so close to You and
share in Your special, dearly won life. Amen."

Study Guide

1. What effect has seeing yourself as the center of your universe had on your spiritual growth?
2. What thoughts and feelings come to your mind when you realize that Jesus may want you to be a part of His life as much as or more than you may want Him to be a part of your life?
3. Have you ever had the experience of a Bible passage coming alive to you? What feelings did that experience generate in you?
4. Do you agree with the statement that Jesus suffered every temptation that all human beings suffer? Explain your answer. What feelings does that statement generate in you, especially as you consider the temptations in your own life of which you are most ashamed?
5. How do you think seeing yourself actually involved in an event of Jesus' life will change your perception of yourself?

Suggested Reading

Linn, Dennis, S.J., and Linn, Matthew, S.J. *Healing Life's Hurts.* New York: Paulist Press, 1978.
———. *Healing of Memories.*
Puhl, Louis J., S.J., trans. *The Spiritual Exercises of St. Ignatius.* Chicago: Loyola University Press, 1951.

Chapter 10
Focusing on a Feeling

Many people find the world of feelings to be a dark and discouraging world within them, a world of unknowns, a world in which they feel like a child who is lost and wandering, and therefore a world they would rather avoid. Others, while they are more-or-less comfortable with feelings in general, find certain feelings almost impossible to express or even acknowledge. Surely, accepting one's feelings is something many modern people need to learn to do.

It is important that we learn to do so because feelings are at the heart of where we live. Our thoughts may guide us, our attitudes and opinions may limit or focus us, our decisions may rule out other options and give our lives direction, but our feelings, as Conrad Baars says, are our motors, our motivators. Feelings give us the energy we need to live life fully. This is one reason that when we begin to run from our feelings, to pretend they are not what they are, and to repress them into unconsciousness, we usually become either depressed or sick—a state opposite to that of spiritual growth.

Immediately, however, we must distinguish between a Christian approach to feelings and approaches that are common today in the world at large. We are not claiming that people should act on all their feelings, say anything that comes into their minds, or let their lives be controlled by feelings as the modern slogans "Do your own thing" and "If it feels good, do it" suggest. No, a Christian approach and the approach of responsible schools of psychology is that we acknowledge all our feelings, feel them fully, and then decide with some moral code what we shall do with them. Therefore, in this chapter we shall investigate how we might get in touch with our feelings in a Christian way so that we can use these "motors" as energy in our quest for spiritual growth and healing.

General Principles

When we look at our feelings as the motors of our lives, we need not worry that, for example, a feeling of anger acknowledged and felt will motivate us with energy only to be angry. Once the energy is released by acknowledging the feeling consciously, the energy is at our disposal to use as we see fit. We can decide to use the energy released by feeling anger, for example, to express love. This is the point of decision at which our moral code is all-important, for by it we will determine how to use the energy within us: to build or destroy, to plant or uproot. At various times any of those choices may be morally correct and even imperative, and our understanding of morality will guide our decision concerning what to do in a concrete situation.

Because we are often afraid of our feelings and of the power they have, we are often tempted to repress them, that is, to leave them unacknowledged. Doing this, however, only further confuses us and even leads us into sin. For when we repress a feeling it does not disappear, but sinks into unconsciousness where it is still active but out of our control.

When we repress an angry feeling, for example, it does not cease making us feel angry, but we have given up our ability to direct that anger to do something creative with it—a choice we could have made if we had first decided to acknowledge and feel the anger. Many times we repress our emotions because we do not want to face the responsibility of making a moral decision concerning how to use the energy it will release in us. Making that moral decision would be, however, an important step in our spiritual growth.

Furthermore, that unconscious angry feeling will somehow find a way to be expressed without benefit of the light of consciousness, and therefore it will result in some form of unwholesome behavior. It may be expressed in the form of backbiting, slander, sarcasm, judgment, condemnation, building walls in relationships, bitterness, in some expression of anger toward self like depression, or even after a while it may build up to verbal or physical violence. These reactions are the necessary consequence of repressing emotions like anger, and they are the very opposite of the spiritual growth we seek.

The Scriptures also urge us to this kind of emotional honesty because it is spiritually as well as psychologically healthy. In his Letter to the Ephesians, Paul gives practical advice on handling, as an example, our anger. He begins by explaining our responsibility to tell the truth to each other (in psychological terms we would say we should not repress our true thoughts but rather find an acceptable way to express them): "So from now on, there must be no more lies: you must speak the truth to one another since we are all parts of one another" (4:25). And he links that idea immediately with being honest about difficult emotions like anger, for in the next sentence he says: "Even if you are angry you must not sin: never let the sun set on your anger or else you will give the devil a foothold" (4:26).

So Paul is saying that the way we sin with our anger is by keeping it inside us longer than to the end of that day on which we first felt it. We must find a way to express our anger or else we are giving the devil a foothold. A foothold to what, we may ask? We are giving him a foothold in our lives to accomplish all the works of repressed anger we discussed just two paragraphs above. Those sins will come as a necessary consequence to "letting the sun set on" our anger.

But Paul continues, saying that there are limits on how we can *express* that anger: "Never have grudges against others, or lose your temper, or raise your voice to anybody, or call each other names, or allow any sort of spitefulness" (4:31). Often, when we resist the notion of acknowledging and feeling all of our feelings, it is not because the feeling is "wrong" (no feelings are wrong, they just are; what we do with them may be right or wrong), but because when we think of the feeling, in this case, anger, we judge it by its companions or by the way we have expressed it in the past. If our anger is usually accompanied by spitefulness or name-calling or screaming, it is the companions we are judging to be wrong, not the anger itself. Our expression of feelings may need to be redirected, but acknowledging our feelings and expressing them properly will always be necessary to psychological health and spiritual growth.

When we pray to accept our feelings, then, we are praying to come in touch with our true selves. Often the revelation of our true selves will be a surprise to us, but a necessary one. Also, when we pray to accept our feelings, we put ourselves in touch with memories in which those feelings played a part, for rarely do we have a feeling that is not associated with one or several memories. Therefore, we examine acknowledging our feelings in conjunction with healing of memories because doing so is another avenue to spiritual growth.

So we bring our emotions out of darkness and into the Light of Christ where they can be healed. Then a simplicity comes to be a part of us—a part of the way we choose to live— that allows us to say what we mean and to mean what we say. Once we begin to live in that way we find that we are able to talk with God in prayer and hear His response (Chapter 2), and we are able to talk with other people and, if not communicate with them (for communication is two-way), at least understand our dialogue with them.

Jesus needs men and women of honesty and morality to be His ambassadors in the world (2 Cor 5:20). How can we help the world to see that Christ has reconciled the world to Himself if we are not reconciled to ourselves? How can we tell the world that Christ does not condemn them if we condemn ourselves and our emotions? By being men and women who choose to grow spiritually, we become agents of His healing love and we are able to do the work of Christ in the world.

A Description of the Prayer

I was introduced to this way of praying by my friends Dennis and Matthew Linn. We begin to pray to focus on a feeling by first asking Christ to be with us, for we would not want to come into contact with any powerful emotion if we were not secure in the Love of Christ. We ask Jesus to bless us, to bless the place in which we are praying, and to protect us and support us so that we can touch the depth of our feelings without fear of being lost in them or controlled by them. If we place ourselves trustingly in the hands of Christ at the beginning of this prayer, we are assured that the results of the prayer will be healing for us.

Next, praying and under the guidance of the Spirit, we choose a feeling we need to accept more completely. Many people find it helpful in learning to accept a feeling to experience it first as a bodily reaction. While some are at first too inhibited to do this, maybe these people are the ones who would benefit from it the most, for it would bring their bodies, minds, and spirits into a greater unity, and thus make them more whole. To acknowledge a feeling bodily, we focus our minds on the feeling (for example, fear) and we ask ourselves: "When I am afraid, how does my body react to fear? What muscles become tense? Do aches or pains come into any particular parts of my body? How would I express fear by using my body, that is, what position of my hands, arms, legs, torso, and head would be a 'picture' or 'sculpture' of this feeling to me?"

Then we crawl into the feeling by allowing ourselves to remember those bodily reactions to fear, or by creating a "picture" of fear by positioning our bodies in a way that would express fear. If we have never tried an exercise like this before, we may think it childish, lacking in dignity, or more appropriate for people "who like to do that sort of thing"; but we will probably be surprised, if we try it once or twice, how it helps us to feel our feelings deeply. Since feelings are both psychological and physical, we need to remember our bodily reactions if we are to come fully in contact with a particular feeling. Once we are fully in touch with a feeling, we can fully give it to Jesus for healing.

Next, we examine the psychological level of this feeling. We ask ourselves: "What thoughts do I have when I feel this feeling? Do any other feelings accompany it? How do I want to act when I have this feeling?" Again, we take the time to allow those very thoughts to come into our minds, for, we remember, we are praying and in the presence of Christ; and when we allow these thoughts and feelings to enter our minds where Christ has first been invited, what we are doing is confessing these thoughts and feelings to Him. It is only when we focus on these feelings alone or only in the presence of another and not also in the presence of our healing God that we can get ourselves into trouble by acting on our feelings rashly, or by being engulfed in the disease of introspection. When we are able to be honest with Jesus, however, we place in His hands the feeling that needs His touch, and He has then been freed by a decision of our own wills to be able to heal us.

We continue to come in contact with this feeling at a psychological level by asking ourselves in the presence of Jesus if there are any events that are examples of times when this feeling came on us with particular intensity. We take enough time at this point to allow those memories to come forth. Again, as we learned in the last two chapters, we want to allow the Holy Spirit complete control over releasing memories from our unconscious minds into our conscious minds, for when He is in control, neither will an appropriate situation for healing be missed nor will we unearth something too powerful to handle. We trust Him to do the most loving thing that can be done for us at this moment and to remain with us to the conclusion of the prayer to assist us in dealing with that for which we need healing.

At this point in the prayer, we may make a choice, if not to do one of these things *or* the other, at least to determine which of them we will do first. Whether or not any memories have come forth, we may feel the need to pray for a simple healing for the emotional state in which we now find ourselves in the presence of Christ. Knowing that we have felt this way many times before and that our inability to understand and direct these feelings has led us to great unfreedom, we may want to pray simply to ask the Holy Spirit to comfort us, strengthen us, reveal to us the good uses to which this feeling may be directed, and show us a way out of any "blind alleys" in relationships into which these feelings have led us in the past.

Another option, if some memories have come forth, is to pray for healing of memories by seeing Christ in these events of our lives, as we learned in Chapter 8. In doing so, we continue to be honest with the Lord about our feelings in these situations, but as we see Him in these situations we observe carefully what He says and does, how He treats us and others, and what He asks us to do to resolve the situations. We open ourselves to all the love and comfort He is desiring to give to us to heal the hurt in these events, and we open ourselves to change our attitudes toward others as He directs us.

A third option is to pray healing of memories by seeing ourselves in the events of Christ's life. Acting on this choice, we ask ourselves at what times in Jesus' life did He seem to feel the same way that we felt in our memory. If it is possible to look up the Scripture passage that describes the event, we do so; we divide it into a beginning, middle, and end and enter each section of the story in all the ways we investigated in Chapter 9. If we find ourselves wondering whether Jesus ever felt things like fear, anger, shame, bitterness, and so forth, we remember that as a human being He had a full complement of human emotions, trials, and sufferings (Heb 4:12–5:10), and if we cannot find a passage in which He seems to express the feelings that we have had, we can look to His Passion and Death, in which He suffered not for His own life but for all of ours. In that story we will see Jesus identifying with our lives completely, except for committing sin Himself. But even on that subject, while He did not experience the pain of sinning Himself, He did experience our sin within Him.

As we pray in this way, then, we identify with Jesus' point of view on this feeling. We ask Him to enter our hearts so as to teach us gently how we can make His way our own. We ask forgiveness for all the times we have misunderstood this feeling in the past and therefore have judged ourselves, and we ask forgiveness for all the times we have misused this feeling and hurt others (Chapter 5).

Finally, we pray for peace to surround us and fill us. We ask Him to show us a new way to live while being more aware and respectful of our feelings, and to show us how to use our feelings to build His Kingdom.

An Example

Several years ago I prayed this prayer with a young lady who, after several sessions, revealed that when she was a girl of ten or eleven she endured an agonizing night during which her mother attempted to commit suicide. Since this was obviously a key memory, I knew we had to pray about it, but first we investigated all the ways in which this event had colored her life after it happened. We especially saw how the paralyzing fear that gripped her adult life in moments of crisis had its roots in this night of terror. We saw how every time she faced a difficult encounter like a confrontation with her husband she clenched with the same paralyzing fear she felt on that dreadful night.

After seeing the meaning of the event in her present life, we began to pray about it by focusing on the feeling of fear. I prayed that Jesus would be present to both of us, and then I asked her to remember that night and recall the feeling of fear she had—to remember how her stomach felt, her back, her neck—and then also to recall how fear felt in her body in crises in her adult life. Then she began remembering the thoughts she experienced on that night as a child. She remembered hearing the screams of her mother, the sounds of struggle between her mother and father, and the sense of the hopelessness of it all.

She remembered lying on her bed, afraid to get up and see what was happening, afraid that if she did not do something the worst would happen, and feeling forced to listen to those horrifying screams with her heart reaching out to her mother and hating her mother at the same time. She realized that in that moment of terrifying pain she had decided to cut off many of her feelings toward her mother, simply because it was too painful to continue to acknowledge her feelings toward her.

That in itself was a shocking realization and it would have

been impossible to bear had Jesus not been with us. I prayed, asking Him to be one with this woman as He suffered paralyzing fear in Gethsemane. At once she found herself next to the Lord in that garden experiencing a terrible wrenching in His body and spirit, while she also sensed profoundly His presence with her in her bedroom sharing her pain, loneliness, and terror as a child. After giving an appropriate time to this prayer, and after a significant emotional release in her own screaming and tears, she knew that her pain was being redeemed by her Lord.

Then there came into her mind other times in which she had felt this same paralyzing fear—not exactly particular events, but more general times in her life that were marked by a sense of anxiety and terror. As she concentrated on these feelings in the presence of Jesus, He again helped her to bring them into Gethsemane and to suffer them alongside Him. In each instance, His strength to live through the moment of ultimate terror filled her entire being and won a victory—not, of course, without the price of feeling the pain this one last time—over the fear of her life. We concluded the prayer by extending forgiveness to her mother and father, and to all those who had been a part of each situation that had made her afraid. Finally we prayed that she forgive herself for giving into the fear and not looking to Jesus to help her a long time ago.

The prayer itself was cathartic and beautiful, and she felt free. But the proof of Jesus' healing her came when several weeks later she and her husband argued over something important, and, in a situation in which she would in the past have been paralyzed by fear, she stood her ground without overstating her case on the one hand, and without forgoing her principles on the other. Truly, Jesus' strength had become so much a part of her that He freed her to be a new woman, to feel and act on her own dignity, and to love others even when she and they were in conflict.

A Sample Prayer

This prayer will focus on feelings of joy and fear, although it could focus on any emotions. When we pray this kind of prayer in our own words, we need to ask the Spirit to show us on which feeling we need to focus. Before we begin this sample prayer, we need to review the four steps by which we enter into a state of prayer, which were outlined in the section of the Preface entitled "A Note on Using the Sample Prayers in This Book." Once we have prepared ourselves in this way, we can begin to pray.

"Thank You, Jesus, that You are so willing and able to share my feelings with me. Thank You for this opportunity to confess honestly in Your presence the feelings of my life and what I have done with them. I open myself entirely to You now, Lord. Let me be aware with a heightened sensitivity of Your presence within and around me. Bless me, Lord, and bless the place in which I now pray. Let your holy Light fill this place and consume all darkness within it. And may Your light fill me with peace.

"Holy Spirit, come to me now in a special way to guide this prayer. Help me to be sensitive to my deepest needs and to Your deepest desires for me. At each point in the prayer, show me what You would have me do to bring about Jesus' will for me.

"Lord Jesus, help me to focus on the emotion of joy in my life. Help me first to come in touch with the ways in which joy affects my body. How does my body feel when I am joyful? Which muscles respond to this emotion, which organs, which limbs? Do any particular physical sensations become apparent to me, for example, in my head or in my stomach? Help me to listen to my body now as it tells me how I feel joy. . . .

"Similarly, Jesus, help me to be one with my body to find out how it would express joy in a physical 'picture.' What position of my body (e.g., standing, sitting, etc.), what position of my arms (e.g., raised, lowered, straight, bent, etc.), what position of my legs, hands, and head would express joy as I feel it? Let me respond in Your Spirit to these questions, so that I may

*become totally open to all that You would do within
me during this prayer."*

We now take the time necessary to respond to these questions in action and to feel the feeling of joy within us. After we
have given this part of the prayer a due amount of time, we
continue.

*"Lord, help me to look within myself now to all the
reactions that accompany joy when I feel it. What
thoughts do I have when I feel joy? How do I want to
act when I feel this way? Help me to answer these
thoughts honestly in Your presence, so that You can
help me to derive every drop of life that I can receive
from my joyful experiences and feelings. . . .*

*"Jesus, reveal to me any significant moments of joy
in my life that You want me to remember at this time.
Help me to remember these events in all their details
and to share them now with You. . . .*

*"Help me to remember, Lord, the times You felt
joyful and to unite myself with You in those times.
Maybe I can identify best with the dancing and feast-
ing at the wedding feast in Cana (Jn 2:1–12), or with the
spiritual joy You felt when Peter confessed You as the
Messiah (Mt 16:13–20), or the joy You felt when You
were with the little children (Mk 10:13–16). Guide me,
Jesus, to chooose one of these or another passage of
Scripture in which I can know the fullness of Your joy
in my heart."*

We take time now to look up a Scripture passage and,
following the guidelines we discovered in Chapter 9, we pray
seeing ourselves in this event from the life of Jesus. When we
have completed this part, we continue.

*"Thank You, Jesus, for letting me share that experience
with You. It gives me great confidence to know that*

*You and I can share human life so intimately. But,
Lord, this feeling of joy is strange to me, maybe because I find it difficult so often to feel joyful about
myself and life. More often than not I am afraid instead. Let me be aware of how strongly You are within
me, giving me the courage to face myself in my weakness.*

"*Lord, help me to get in touch with the fear within me by feeling it in my body now. How does my
body feel when I am afraid? Which muscles respond to
this feeling, which organs, which limbs? Do any particular physical sensations become apparent to me, for
example, in my stomach, back, or head? Help me to
listen to my body now as it tells me how I experience
fear. . . .*

"*Also, Lord, help me to get in touch with my fear
by allowing my body to express a 'picture' of it. With
my hands and arms, legs and feet, torso and head, let
me express how I feel when I feel fear. . . . I do this in
Your presence, Jesus, as a gift to You in trust, doing all
I can to open myself to You that You are free to heal
me.*

"*Jesus, help me to be honest now about the psychological effects that fear has on me. What thoughts
come to my mind when I feel afraid? Help me to tell
them to You right now. . . . How do I want to act when
I feel afraid? Help me to confess those thoughts to You
right now. . . . In being honest with You, Jesus, I know
that I am choosing to let You heal me. Thank You.*

"*Lord, although You never gave in to fear, still
there were times when other people or circumstances
tried to make You feel afraid. Help me to identify with
You when it seemed that the boy You had delivered of
demons was dead (Mk 9:14–29), or when You foretold
Your suffering and death and Peter disagreed with You
(Mt 16:21–23), or when You spent the night in Gethsemane knowing what would happen the next day (Lk*

22:39–46). Or help me to identify with You as You carried the fears of all people in Your Cross and were nailed to that Cross by sins.

"As I enter Your experience with You, relying on Your word that says that You live in me and I live in You, let the strength, confidence, and identity You have as the Son of God flow into me and change my reaction to the fear I am tempted to feel.... Let me know that because You are with me I need not be afraid, for Your Love consumes all fear.... Let Your point of view become my point of view. Let Your healing Love be the power that changes my heart into Yours, and teaches me to respond to situations as You did."

We now take the time to look up one of the suggested Scripture passages or another that may come to mind, and we pray to see ourselves in this event in the life of Christ (Chapter 9). We take the time necessary to finish this part of the prayer completely, and then we conclude.

"Thank You, Jesus, for freeing me through Your experience. Thank You for the new life I now have in You. Thank You for the new possibilities my future now holds because I have in one more part of my life identified with You. This spiritual growth is a treasure in my heart.

"Again, Lord, I ask for peace and protection for those sensitive parts of me that You have healed in this prayer. Let them grow strong in your Love before they are tested. And show me how I may use them to be a more active and creative witness to Your Love and a more energetic builder of Your Kingdom in the world in which I live. Amen."

Study Guide

1. How have the modern slogans "Do your own thing" and "If it feels good, do it" affected your spiritual growth?
2. Do you tend to repress your feelings and emotions, or do you tend to express them? Give an example, or explain your answer.
3. How have you understood St. Paul's words about anger in Eph 4:25–31 in the past? Do you need to change your understanding, and, if so, how?
4. How do you see the differences among anger, the companions of anger, and the ways you express anger in your life?
5. How do you think learning to accept all your feelings will bring spiritual growth into your life? What are some of the principles you use in deciding to express your feelings once you feel them?

Suggested Reading

Baars, Conrad W. *Feeling and Healing Your Emotions.* Plainfield, N.J.: Logos International, 1979.

Linn, Dennis, S.J., and Linn, Matthew, S.J. *Healing Life's Hurts.* New York: Paulist Press, 1978.

Tapscott, Betty. *Set Free.* Houston, TX: Hunter Books, 1978.

Other Suggested Reading

Baars, Conrad W. *Born Only Once.* Chicago: Franciscan Herald Press, 1975.

Faricy, Robert, S.J. *Praying for Inner Healing.* New York: Paulist Press, 1980.

Feider, Paul A. *The Christian Search for Meaning in Suffering.* West Mystic, CN.: Twenty-Third Publications, 1981.

Scanlon, Michael. *Inner Healing.* New York: Paulist Press, 1974.

Shlemon, Barbara, Linn, Dennis, S.J., and Linn, Matthew, S.J. *To Heal as Jesus Healed.* Notre Dame, IN: Ave Maria Press, 1978.

Wead, Douglas. *The Compassionate Touch.* Carol Stream, IL: Creation House, 1977.

Appendices

Appendix A
On Applying These Prayers to
General Healing Services

General healing services are becoming more and more common today in a variety of religious settings. From formal church congregations to informal gatherings like prayer meetings and study groups, people who come together to find God want to discover His healing Love, and they find their group setting a supportive place in which to make this discovery.

Furthermore, general healing services, while they cannot entirely replace individual prayer or one-to-one ministry, can be effective for many people in need of healing. While notable people like Agnes Sanford in her most recent book *Creation Waits* (Logos, 1978) offer some cautions regarding general prayers for inner healing (mainly pointing out the need for follow-up for the people who are deeply moved at such services), general healing services have been a part of many different Christian traditions as a means of spiritual growth. The faith and love of all who are gathered at a service is so much more than the faith and love of one or two alone, and it often is the case that the greater the faith and love present, the more mightily God can work.

This book has been written with readers in mind who want to pray for inner healing for themselves. This appendix is meant to help readers who want to apply some of these ideas to develop general healing services. Each chapter of the book focuses on a different kind of prayer for inner healing, and the sample prayers at the end of each chapter are meant to give readers an idea of how a prayer like the one described in that chapter would sound. These prayers could serve both as a beginning of personal prayer for inner healing and as the beginning of a general prayer for inner healing, except the prayer for deliverance (Chapter 6), which should *never* be prayed in a group because, as that chapter emphasizes, the proper setting, time, and internal disposition for a successful deliverance are different for every individual. We must always remember how delicate deliverance is and how easy it is to be harmed by it when it is not done in a way that is sensitive to a person's needs and individuality.

Applying the Prayers

Prayer, especially prayer for inner healing, is a personal experience. In this kind of prayer, people who pray want to integrate the experience of prayer with their own hearts. When one person prays with another, the person who is praying needs to be sensitive to the other, and the person for whom the prayer is being prayed needs to accept that prayer within, allowing the words to touch and move the heart.

The issue, then, of exactly what should be said during an inner healing prayer is an extremely sensitive one. We need above all to keep this point in mind as we investigate the possibility of using written prayers in general services of healing. As I have already mentioned in the Preface, I think that when praying for inner healing it is best if we can compose our own prayers, not being self-conscious and thinking about our eloquence or lack thereof, but rather praying from the heart and responding to the needs in this unique time and place of the person(s) for whom we are praying—ourselves, another individual, or a group of people.

However, not everyone is always able to do the best thing in every situation. If we are not able to compose a prayer in our own words because of feelings of insecurity, lack of emotional sensitivity, inexperience, or the like, that does not mean that

God cannot use us to minister to others. When I first began to pray with others, it took everything within me just to have the faith in God to suggest prayer ministry and to follow through by praying; there was literally no energy within me left with which to be original in my prayer. At those times I mimicked my teacher in prayer, Barbara Shlemon: I remembered what she had said in similar situations and repeated those words as exactly as I could. Later, however, as I became more confident in myself and in my faith in a God Who heals, I did find within myself the freedom to compose my own prayers. While God worked through many of those early prayers, the difference between them and the ones I composed myself was that the latter were more powerful prayers.

It seems to me that one of the reasons original prayers can have more power is that we are more involved in them, and therefore more of our faith, hope, and love go into them. If God, Who is creative, made us in His own image and likeness, He expects us to explore our own creativity to its limits and thereby give Him praise. While not all of us are artistic, eloquent, musical, or work well with our hands, all of us can be creative in our living and in our praying. These are the simplest and most basic areas of creativity, and we can strive to explore our creative drives within them.

Before I wrote the sample prayers in this book, I prayed that the words I would write would touch the hearts of those who would read and pray them. Therefore, I know in faith that God will work through them to help others. But the reader must not believe that just because a prayer is in print it is the best prayer that could be prayed. The best prayer that can be prayed is one that responds uniquely to the situation and to the people for whom it is prayed.

It is my hope, then, that if people use these prayers for general healing services, they will consider using them as models and not as acutal prayers. To do this they can read the prayer, study it, compare it with the description of the prayer found within the chapter, and try to make it so much their own that they could with some ease pray a similar prayer in their own words. In this way as ministers of prayer to others, they

will be open to the special guidance of the Holy Spirit to
respond to the unique needs of the people for whom they pray
at that time, while if they were reading a written prayer, they
would not be able to respond to those gentle stirrings in their
hearts.

Of course, as with most things, there are many ways to
accomplish this goal, and there are many ways to compromise
between the two extremes of reading a prayer on the one hand
and composing an original prayer on the other. One compromise, which might meet many of the needs of those who will
receive the prayer as well as acknowledge the possible self-
consciousness and anxiety of the person who would minister to
them, would be to read a prayer slowly and meditatively, stop-
ping after each paragraph, listening within for any guidance
that the Holy Spirit may give, verbalizing those prayers as He
gives them with faith that they will meet the individual needs of
those present. To pray in this way both gives freedom to the
Spirit to speak through us the words that are needed for particular people in a unique time and space and acknowledges our
own limitations in praying.

Another way to combine the ideas of preparation and spon-
taneity is to study the kind of prayer that we want to pray with
others, develop an outline of the points that seem to be essential
to the prayer, and use that written outline as we pray in our
own words. A third way to accomplish this end is to have two or
three people prepare together to pray the prayer. Agreeing
beforehand on the purpose of the prayer and the general area it
will cover, they stand before the group. First one prays as the
Spirit leads, and when that person's inspiration ceases another
takes over; the two or three alternate praying in this way until
the area is covered. For this last method, it is important that the
people who pray together have a spiritual unity between/among
them (not necessarily an emotional friendship, but a spiritual
sense of oneness) and that one of them is the acknowledged
leader of the group who would both begin and end the prayer. I
myself have used all three of these ways of praying with groups
and have found them each extremely successful, but only, of
course, when the Holy Spirit guides me to use them.

Finally, we must caution readers who are not the acknowledged leaders of the group for whom they wish to pray this prayer: these readers need to develop their plans in conjunction with the leader of the group. Inner healing prayers do not work well when they are surprises; neither are surprises submissive to the spiritual authority of the leader. But when there is loving and gentle preparation, inner healing prayers communicate the Love of God not only in the words used but also in the manner in which the prayer is presented to the group. And we must always remember: It is the Love of God that heals, not our words or ideas, and especially not our schemes.

Developing a General Healing Service

The simpler the general service of healing is, in general, the better it will be. While, if we are praying over and over again with the same group, it is good once in a while to add a unique element to our prayer—for example, to make a service appropriate to a special occasion—it is in a simple service that God is most free to move. This does not mean that we cannot be creative or inventive in developing general healing services, only that it is best not to become too complicated.

We also need to acknowledge the limitations we have and to use the gifts that are available to us. For example, if we can work with a musical group that is spiritually sensitive and musically accomplished, then we ought to allow music a larger role in the service than if our musical resources are sparse. If we have available to us a person who is intuitively capable of finding symbols to express ideas and thus create exciting liturgical experiences, we would do best to rely on that person's creativity. If there is no one in our group who has experience praying inner healing prayers, we should not demand of ourselves that someone pray an entirely spontaneous general prayer for inner healing.

There are, however, some common elements to most services of inner healing. One is that the group with whom the prayer is prayed is prepared several weeks in advance, or through publicity, that a general prayer for inner healing will be prayed at a particular gathering of the group. Doing this helps people to come anticipating the experience of receiving the Lord's healing Love.

Religious music is also a common element—live, recorded, or both. If good musical resources are available to us, music can help people praise God and enter into a state of prayer; it can punctuate a general healing prayer itself (songs appropriate to a particular part of the prayer played after that part of the prayer has been prayed), thus giving people a new medium through which to let the Lord heal them; it can be a part of the service that stimulates people to recognize their need for healing or teaches them about what healing can do; it can help conclude a service with peace and joy.

Prayers preparatory to the general healing prayer are also helpful. They help people to ready themselves for what is to come by praising God for His goodness. They also create a spiritually safe atmosphere in which to pray. As we ask the Light of God to fill the room in which we pray, as we ask for the protection of the angels, as we pray that God send His Spirit deeply into our hearts to reveal what He wants healed in us at this moment, as we praise God for being God, we are coming more personally in touch with the One Who will heal us.

Some form of teaching on inner healing, what it is and what it can do, not only instructs people but also encourages them to the virtue of hope for healing. Furthermore, it stimulates some of us to recognize in a deeper way our personal need for healing (something from which we often hide because it is too threatening). This teaching can be given personally by someone in the group. While it is not highly recommended because it can more easily lose people's interest, the teaching could be in the form of a tape recording. An excellent and interesting way to teach about healing is to use one of the many films about healing that are available.[1]

Many healing services also include one or two witnesses by people who have been healed. This element is especially helpful if these people were healed through the prayer of this very group on another occasion, or at least in a situation with which most of the people in the group are familiar. These stories should be concise and concrete. These witness stories build the faith of those who hear them if they are simple, not overdone, and do not attract attention away from God and to the person who tells them.

Just before the general prayer for inner healing is prayed, it is good to instruct people on some points about entering into prayer and, specifically, into inner healing prayer. First, some people need to know that inner healing prayer uses the imagination, but that imagination does not necessarily mean visualizing (points more fully explained in the Preface). They need to know that imagination is the means by which they will enter into the prayer and make it their own.

Many people are awed or frightened by the possibility of reacting emotionally to prayer in a group situation. The leader can put people at ease by saying that emotional responses are neither desirable nor undesirable, that the prayer can be healing for them with or without emotional displays. However, if emotional responses do come forth spontaneously, it is best for us not to stifle them but to express them freely. While many people, when they do respond emotionally, respond in tears, some respond in joy and laughter; and when we pray we need to trust that, if we are allowing the Spirit to be in charge of the situation, whatever response (or lack of response) comes is the best possible way that the Spirit can work with us at this time to heal us. Emotional catharsis is important for some kinds of healing, while it is not all that important for other kinds.

If some people in the group are new to inner healing prayer, they need to be told they can pray the prayer for themselves rather than for another. Some people have the mistaken notion that it is selfish to pray for themselves. Others often feel moved to pray for people close to them, like their own children, because, for example, through teaching on inner healing they have come to see that they have hurt their children deeply. However, praying out of guilt is not often successful, and people in this situation need to know that the best thing they can do for their children is to be healed themselves, so that they can react to their children in a healed and healing way in the future.

Finally, we remind the group that, since someone is praying with them and leading them in prayer, they need not so
much exert an effort to pray or to do something in prayer as
much as to relax and flow with the prayer, allowing the powerful Love of God to saturate them.

Then, to begin the prayer, we use the four preparatory
steps to prayer outlined in the section of the Preface entitled "A
Note on Using the Sample Prayers in This Book," that is,
become comfortable and sit up straight, focus our attention on
God, regulate and slow down our breathing, and let go of any
distractions that may come into our minds. At this point the
leader remains in silence for awhile to allow each heart to come
into the Spirit, especially his or her own, and to come in touch
with any spiritual intuitions for the prayer that the Spirit may
be offering in guidance. Then, aloud, the leader begins by
thanking God for this opportunity, for all the people, and for all
the problems that bring us to God for help.

The body of the prayer follows, and the leader prays it
(alone or with the assistance of one or two persons) in a manner
that has been selected previously, that is, spontaneously, from
an outline, using a written prayer by itself or with additional
points added spontaneously under the guidance of the Spirit. If
the prayer is read, it is important to read it slowly and meditatively, pausing after each paragraph to allow the group to experience what the prayer describes. If one of the sample prayers
from this book is used, it should be noted that a sequence of
several periods within a paragraph (...) is a signal for a
moment of silence.

If we plan to pray the prayer spontaneously, the most
important point to remember, after we have studied this kind of
prayer and understand what is the object and method of the
prayer, is to listen attentively as we pray to the Holy Spirit for
guidance. To be able to hear Him clearly, we need to turn our
minds and spirits over to Him for His use entirely during this
prayer. Often I do this by praying a prayer in my heart that He
fill me with all the gifts I need to pray the perfect prayer He
wants prayed for these people at this time. Then I relax and give
up any effort to force the prayer or to control it, so I can trust

that whatever comes into my mind is an answer to my request, that is, that what comes into my mind are His thoughts and His guidance at that moment.

If we are planning to pray an entirely spontaneous prayer of inner healing for the first time in our lives, it might relieve some of our anxiety to have an outline of this kind of prayer nearby, just in case we become so self-conscious that nothing of significance comes into our minds. But I have found that if God has led me to do anything new, and if I have done the preparation He has asked of me, when I walk (or talk) in faith He will supply the abilities, the words, or whatever is needed to make His project successful. We must remember and keep our faith that God wants people healed more than we do, that He is the healer and not we, and that He uses best His servants of humble origins.

We can conclude our prayer with a quiet religious song. I find it best at this time not to sing a song for which people need accompaniment or printed words or music, for all of these can distract people and disturb those deeply caught up in prayer. Not everyone has to sing; the song could even be a solo if someone with a good quality voice is available to sing it; it also could be a recording (again, for the sake of not disturbing people's prayer, the turntable or tape recorder needs to be so arranged that it can be turned on and off without fuss, mistakes, or extraneous noises; it should be a recording of good quality so that people can clearly understand any words). A period of silence, from two to five minutes, is also appropriate at this time. In some situations it is important to allow the place in which the prayer has been prayed to remain in silence for a longer period of time. If silence seems to be appropriate after a particular prayer, we can ask those who finish praying sooner than others to leave that room and gather for fellowship and conversation elsewhere.

I am sure that these are not all the reflections that would be helpful to someone planning a service of general healing, but these are points that I have found to be helpful when I have prayed in this way. As we use these suggestions we need to adapt them to our own situations so as to make them helpful to our group, and not use them rigidly. Most of all, we need to plan our service for general healing in the faith, hope, and love through which God heals.

Note

1. These movies are available from CharCom Productions, Inc., Merton House, 4453 MacPherson, St. Louis, MO 63108. Purchase prices, rental fees, shipping fees and other information are available from them.

1. *The Power of Healing Prayer.* This film shows a scientifically controlled experiment at St. Vincent Hospital and Medical Center in Toledo, OH, in which twenty-four patients who had been selected by a team of doctors as having diseases medical science cannot cure are prayed with over a three-day period by a team comprising Francis MacNutt, Paul Schaaf, Jeanne Hill, and Barbara Shlemon. Twenty-one out of the twenty-four patients show significant improvement in the eyes of the doctor who is controlling the study, and he says that he can attribute these changes to no medical treatment but to the prayer prayed with these people; along the way a simple method for praying healing prayer is explained. ($28\frac{1}{2}$ minutes)

2. *Teaching Series #1, Francis MacNutt.* Francis MacNutt, internationally known for his healing ministry, discusses healing and the lost heritage of prayer in the Church. (20 minutes)

3. *Teaching Series #2, Barbara Shlemon.* Mrs. Shlemon, a wife, mother, and registered nurse, who has traveled widely in the United States as well as around the world bringing the message of healing to the churches, explains the need for a fuller awareness of the power of prayer by physicians, nurses, and other members of health care teams in their care for the sick. (20 minutes)

4. *Teaching Series #3, Jeanne Hill.* Sr. Jeanne, a powerful and sensitive teacher and minister of healing, explains the dynamics of inner healing. (20 minutes)

Note: From among the above four movies, three or four can be purchased as a package for special rates.

5. *The Power of Forgiveness.* Dennis Linn, S.J., and Matthew Linn, S.J., well-known authors and ministers of healing, explain how the gift of forgiveness from the Holy Spirit enables people to have new freedom and peace in their relationships with themselves and others. (28 minutes)

6. *Simple Ways to Pray.* Dennis Linn, S.J., and Matthew Linn, S.J., explore several creative ways to pray for forgiveness and healing for ourselves and those we love; each is illustrated by individuals actually using these prayer methods. (28 minutes)

7. *New Life through Forgiveness.* Dennis Linn, S.J., interviews a psychiatrist, Bulent Tunakan, M.D., who explains how he discovered the healing power of forgiveness in his battle with cancer; the five stages of dying are compared with the stages of forgiveness. (18 minutes)

8. *The Power of Intercessory Prayer.* Dennis Linn, S.J., and Matthew Linn, S.J., describe the importance of praying for others and tell of the tremendous impact this kind of praying has had on their ministry and their personal lives. (18 minutes)

Note: From among the last four films, two, three, or four can be purchased as a package at special rates.

Appendix B
On Applying These Prayers
to Individual Ministry

Most of the prayers described in this book I came to discover or to make my own as I used them in individual ministry to people in need. My understanding of them evolved as I used them to minister to hurting people, and in this appendix I offer some personal reflections to other people who are involved in a similar ministry, one-to-one, with people who come seeking spiritual growth through inner healing. I suggest, then, that these prayers can be valuable tools for the Christian counselor, psychologist, psychiatrist, social worker, doctor, and nurse, for the priest or minister, and for the lay person in a ministry of healing.

Of necessity, the comments made in this short space will be sketchy; the topic of ministry through prayer to individuals is worthy of an entire book, or even of several. Furthermore, to address in detail an audience so widely divergent as to include both individuals who are highly trained in a particular field like theology or psychology and individuals who became involved in ministry to others through an inner inspiration of the Holy Spirit like a lay minister of healing is difficult indeed. Yet, because these prayers were originally used in individual ministry and are eminently applicable to it, this book would not be complete without some such commentary. It is my hope that, among all the different kinds of people who are interested in praying with individuals in need, these few words will be helpful, will stimulate them to further study, will encourage them to share with others who are interested in prayer ministry both in discussion and in mutual inner healing prayer, and will assist them in their own pursuit of the forms of prayer that are indeed most successful for them as they try to help people who are suffering.

General Principles in Individual Prayer Ministry

Some schools of psychological thought instruct a counselor to be objective and sometimes even distant. Some forms of prayer ministry rely so heavily on spiritual intuition through gifts like discernment and the word of knowledge that the individual in need is only barely consulted regarding the nature and origin of his or her problem. While both of these notions can be valid under certain circumstances, I myself have rarely found them valid when ministering with prayer to a suffering person on a one-to-one basis for inner healing.

For when we minister with inner healing prayer we are entering a God-centered, loving relationship with another person, and while we cannot and do not want to take the place of God, we are in the position of mediating His Love to the person in need. Since God's Love is passionate, concerned, and caring, we who are ministers of His Love cannot be distant or cold in our feelings, our attitudes, or our behavior to the person who comes to us for help. Our attitude must be the attitude of Christ, Who became personally involved with all the people to whom He ministered individually, talking with them, discovering who they were, touching them, caring about what happened to them, speaking for His Father in forgiving them, and doing whatever was necessary to set them free.

We imitate Christ when we listen to the people who come to us for help, when we allow them to express their feelings about the problems that bring them to us, and when we let them know that we personally care about them and about assisting them to find God's help in solving their problems. In doing these things we affirm these people and thus free them to receive more fully the affirming Love of God. In listening carefully to people in need we come to understand what we can do for them and how we can best pray with them.

But we do not receive this information only from the people in front of us. While they are talking to us we are asking God to guide our conversation and to reveal what He sees as the area we can best address with ministry at this moment. We listen within to what He is telling us about these people and about what they need. We also pray actively, but silently, as we listen, asking God to show us how to approach the problem that is being presented to us, what to say by way of comfort and counsel, and how to pray for healing.

We need to be sensitive to the anxiety, fragility, fear, guilt, anger, shyness, and confusion we may find within people who are hurting. We do not want to deny their feelings, disregard them, or discount them; on the other hand, we do not want to give the impression that these feelings are the only reality within this situation, for there is also the reality of Christ, His Love, His ability to redeem the most broken of situations, His kindness and compassion. We are sensitive to the person, and we are also a sign of hope and of Jesus' saving help.

With these general principles in mind, let us look at some of the possible applications of the various prayers described in this book to the work of individual ministry. What follows will not be all of the possible ways in which these prayers can be used, nor is it meant to be a complete list. I do hope that these ideas will stimulate readers who are interested in and called to individual ministry through inner healing to find unique ways to pray with people—ways that only they could discover because they come directly from their unique experience of life.

Prayers to Find Our True Selves

Prayers that aim at finding our true selves are important, and they must not be overlooked in favor of more commonly known inner healing prayers like healing of memories and forgiveness. One of the goals of inner healing is to discover our true selves, and these special ways of praying are powerful toward that end.

Some people come to us with problems relating to the freedom of their intellects, wills, and imaginations. One of many problems could be presented to us: habitual sin, inability to pray because of lack of control of the imagination, inability to think or remember, being painfully distracted by sinful images, rigidity of thought or will, inability to feel emotions or to express them freely—the list could go on. I have often found it helpful to pray with these people to cleanse one or all of the parts of their minds (Chapter 1) and to help them to dedicate their minds to God. Similarly, some people cannot use their imaginations in prayers for healing of memories, for their imaginations are not under their control. Cleansing the imagination begins to free this part of the inner self to be able to function normally again.

Sometimes people seek inner healing because of some habit of sin in their lives. We can work diligently with them to find the sources of this problem and to pray to find a solution through the love of God; but if we do not pray with them also to cleanse their imaginations (Chapter 1) of the memories or images of the times they committed this sin, their minds will continue to be filled with these images, which will tempt them to commit this sin again. Then they will feel guilty and wonder whether God can heal them at all and by losing hope become even more confused. Prayers to cleanse the imagination can help to eliminate this problem.

Often when people come for inner healing ministry they come so confused by the problems of life that they cannot think straight nor can they even hope to hear the still, small voice of God within them, the voice that will give them the answers they seek. One of the greatest gifts we can give to people in these circumstances is to teach them how to listen and how to quiet their inner selves (Chapter 2), and to teach them how to put order into their inner lives through keeping a journal (Chapter 3).

Once these skills are taught and we pray with people for God's grace to fill them so that they can do these things, we have a valuable tool for helping them no matter what the problem they bring to us is. We can also ask them to pray for guidance and to journalize as a kind of "homework" in between sessions with them. People who are involved in and contribute to the process of their own healing are usually healed more quickly and more fully than people who remain passive. Indeed, Jesus in many encounters with the sick either asked them to become involved and to care—to the man at the pool of Bethesda He asked, "Do you want to be well again?" (Jn 5:7)—or He pointed out to them how much their active search for Him and His truth contributed to their healing—"Your faith has restored you to health" (Lk 8:48).

People need to be involved in their own healing to maintain a sense of their own dignity, to see that they as well as the minister of healing stand before God as His children. Learning how to be quiet and listen to God as well as keeping a journal will also give people a sense of security between sessions of healing prayer, for they will come to be able to approach God on their own and ask Him for what they need. Most important, through developing their own personal spiritual lives with these forms of prayer, they will take responsibility for their own lives as Jesus takes on that responsibility with them—"Shoulder my yoke and learn from me" (Mt 11:29); remember, a yoke is made for two—and in doing so they will establish that life-giving connection with Jesus by which they will be healed: "I am the vine, you are the branches. Whoever remains in me, with me in him, bears fruit in plenty . . . if you remain in me and my words remain in you, you may ask what you will and you shall get it" (Jn 15:5a and 7).

When people who are emotionally overwrought come for help, sometimes their condition is the result of not being in emotional balance. In these situations the prayer to integrate opposites within the personality (Chapter 4) can be helpful in resolving their conflicts. When we are out of balance within ourselves we become anxious and often do and say things we easily regret; the prayer of integrating opposites within the personality can be a part of the solution to these problems by bringing peace to a troubled person.

Balancing opposites is often important in marriage counseling, both within each spouse and between them. It is often true that in marriage opposites attract, but when the attraction wears off, the all-important choice between learning from the qualities of the other and resenting them becomes apparent. When wrong choices are made, the individual personalities of both spouses often become crippled and imbalanced. While these kinds of problems cannot in any way be solved with one prayer, a continual praying for integration within each person and for balance within the marriage can be part of the healing process, along with other kinds of counsel and inner healing prayer.

People of great intelligence, people who have been highly educated, and people who have been trained in religious practices that emphasize the ability of will power to free us from sin, or that emphasize the importance of maintaining an intellectually correct truth, have come to me for inner healing; in one way or another they feel frustrated that they are not able to experience God or to express their feelings freely. For these people, their education and/or their religion have bound their intellects and wills—and therefore their imaginations and feelings—instead of freeing them. These people have often put so much effort into developing their intellects and wills that they cannot open them to anyone, not even to God, without new teaching and a great amount of help and encouragement. These people often need prayers of cleansing and dedicating the intellect and the will (Chapter 1) somewhere along the road of healing.

Often, also, these people have so overdeveloped their intellects and wills that they have hidden their imaginations and feelings behind them. In a sense they have misused their intellects and wills to submerge the valid and important function of their minds that is imagination. Thus they need to dedicate their imaginations to God (Chapter 1) as well as to forgive themselves (Chapter 5) as a part of the healing process. They need to put all the functions of their minds into the hands of God that each may be used for the right purposes under the guidance of the Holy Spirit; in this way their emotions will be freed from bondage. However, this is an extremely painful thing for these people to do and cannot be undertaken lightly,

for it will result in a reorientation of their entire lives. Therefore, the minister of healing needs to be sensitive and supportive
while also being firm in pointing out the way to wholeness in
Christ.

Prayers to Free Our True Selves

Prayers that aim at freeing our true selves are necessary
throughout our ministry to most people. They will be a part of
most healing sessions in one form or another. Often they will be
combined with other forms of inner healing prayer to meet all
the needs the person presents to us and to God for healing.

Forgiveness of others, self, and God (not that God is ever
wrong, but sometimes in our eyes He is, and at these times
"forgiving" Him reveals to us our wrong judgment of His
action) is a constant need in our lives. It is therefore often a
component of our prayers in the ministry of inner healing. We
need to remain open to the need to forgive (Chapter 5) as a
possible component to the solution of difficulties both relational
and personal.

Forgiveness prayer can come in many forms, from accepting the faults of self or others, to expressing honestly our anger
toward God and letting Him answer our questions about the
way He is running His universe, to blessing another who hurt
us, to praying for the happiness of the one who hurt us whether
or not our relationship is repaired. Forgiveness radically brings
us into the Kingdom of God and is, therefore, a powerful event
in the process of healing. Furthermore, the message of forgiveness never becomes old (because it is central to the Gospel) and,
therefore, the minister of healing can be confident that, when
the need arises, forgiveness prayer is appropriate, no matter
how many times before the person in need has been asked to
forgive. Forgiveness gives life to the inner self.

Deliverance (Chapter 6) is possibly a part of the healing of
most any situation. When other approaches seem to fail or yield
only limited success, we consider the possibility of the need for
deliverance, while, on the other hand, we never jump to the

conclusion that deliverance is the kind of ministry a particular person needs at a particular time. Most important as we consider this possibility is our ability to hear guidance from the Holy Spirit, for deliverance should never be used when the minister of healing is guided only by human wisdom or knowledge. Only the Spirit can reveal when a person is in need of deliverance, what is the appropriate time, place, and circumstance for the deliverance to take place without harmful side-effects, and what type of deliverance prayer should be used.

In many cases deliverance can and should be prayed silently; in others symbolic language (e.g., Light consuming darkness) ought to be used so as not to frighten the person for whom we pray; in yet others deliverance prayer should be interwoven with prayers for healing of memories or with other forms of inner healing prayer. While all Christians have been given the authority to cast out demons—"These are the signs that will be associated with believers: in my name they will cast out devils" (Mk 16:17)—not many in my experience have the wisdom and are in contact deeply enough with that spiritual authority to cast out demons effectively. When ministering deliverance to others, especially in serious cases, it is best for this prayer to be prayed by a team: one person in authority praying the prayers, another with a tested gift of discernment assisting the first, a third constantly praying prayers of protection and binding of the evil spirits, especially to prevent them from assisting each other, and if others are available they can pray supporting prayer silently in another room.

Satan is overcome by spiritual authority, that is, by being in union with Christ and His power through deep spirituality, prayer, and a life of charity. If we realize that we need to be able to pray for deliverance in our ministry to others, then, we would do best to begin by living the ordinary ways of a dedicated Christian life and by learning from responsible and balanced sources how to minister deliverance prayer with the mind and heart of Christ.

Using religious imagery (Chapter 7) is a deep approach to healing and accomplishes unusually powerful results when guided by the Lord. Healing with this kind of prayer is often at an unconscious level, and it is therefore an approach to keep in mind for deep-seated problems. Again, this prayer would be best used in combination with other prayers of inner healing like healing of memories (Part Three). Because it can heal at levels deeper than many other forms of inner healing prayer, it often follows on them after several sessions with a person with whom we are praying for healing. It is also a good approach to use when the details of a situation needing healing of memories are too complicated to understand and pray about individually. It is a way to mobilize deep energies for health within a person, and so it is helpful in praying for people who are chronically ill or with people who cannot be touched by other forms of inner healing prayer, especially people who resist healing of memories.

Prayers to Heal Our Memories

Because none of us has been perfectly loved or cared for, all of us need healing of memories to one degree or another. This is especially true for those who claim that they do not need this kind of prayer, for by doing so they are only denying their need for love. We must remember, also, that healing of memories is quite often necessary to find the full life-giving energy of our constructive experiences as well as to heal the hurt of our destructive ones.

Often when people come to us in need we can listen to them and with a few questions find that their problem is part of a pattern in their lives. With a little more conversation we can often discover a moment when this pattern in their lives began—what we call a root memory. In this situation praying to see Christ in that event (Chapter 8) is a logical way to approach the situation. This kind of prayer will comfort, support, and encourage these people to believe that God loves them and finds them lovable, and in that awareness and in the power of His Love they are freed not only from the pain of the past but also, in time, from the problem they first presented to us.

Praying to see this event as it relates to a similar event in

Christ's life (Chapter 9) is also a possibility in this situation, although the effect of this prayer is often somewhat different. This kind of prayer gives people a sense of belonging to a mystery much bigger and more important than their own lives, namely, the faith, hope, and love found in the life of Jesus. Thus it is often a more helpful way to pray with people who need to be challenged, confronted with Christ's way of doing things as opposed to their own, gently shocked out of self-pity, or who are so in conflict within themselves that they need to be filled with the mind and attitudes of Christ. This kind of praying is also appropriate for those who are seeking a deeply mystical union with the person and ministry of Christ, as well as for those who are needing that union because they are too caught up in the ways and values of this world. Often a combination of these two ways to pray for healing of memories will be most helpful, and the minister of healing needs to be sensitive and to pray for guidance regarding what to do and what will be the appropriate time in which to do it.

When people who cannot express their feelings come to us for help, or when in the midst of helping a person with other problems we see that, maybe even unconsciously, they are not able to express their true feelings freely, we can pray with them to focus on a feeling (Chapter 10). This prayer is often helpful when combined with other prayers for healing of memories, or with other prayers that free bound emotions like cleansing the imagination (Chapter 1). While chronic depressives fall into this category, before they can be helped by this kind of prayer—which can be quite threatening to them—they often need gentler forms of healing like experiencing a religious image (Chapter 7) in which they are symbolically freed from their depression.

There are many kinds of people for whom a part of their healing will be to come in touch with and identify with the humanity of Jesus. Seeing ourselves in the events of Christ's life (Chapter 9) and focusing on a feeling (Chapter 10) can help us so enter the mind and heart of Jesus that we can see how He faced all the temptations that we have faced. When we enter these situations with Him Who always made the right decisions and never sinned, we can then draw on His strength in temptation through these prayer forms. Thus they are helpful for people who feel particularly weak in any area of their lives.

Guidance and Community in the Ministry of Inner Healing

None of the above ideas should be used in its entirety in the many different situations with which ministers of healing can be faced. These words are only general guidelines, and ones that are bound by the limitations of one person's experiences at that. Therefore, as we pray, we must always rely on the guidance of the Holy Spirit to help us to apply the wisdom we have learned so as to help another person find healing from God. Before we ever begin to pray with anyone in any situation, we must pray for guidance; and once we have asked God to guide our prayer we must pray requesting only that for which we hear in guidance God is telling us to pray. If our prayer for guidance yields only a general notion of how to pray, all we can pray is a general kind of prayer; if our guidance tells us something more specific, we can pray a more specific kind of prayer. The first task of a minister of healing, then, is to learn to hear God and to hear Him clearly (Chapter 2).

While this is a serious responsibility, we must not allow ourselves to become overwhelmed by it. God will work uniquely and powerfully through us if we are dedicated to Him and to His principles of love, and if we give ourselves a chance to minister in His name. He is awaiting our response to His request that we become His healing presence in the world, and there is no prayer He would rather answer than the prayer to help another. We must trust that in His passionate concern for us, His creatures, His general will is that people who are sick will be healed. Supported by His Love, we can do our best to know the things that will be helpful in ministry and to love with all our hearts the people to whom we minister.

If we are to minister to others, if we are to grow in our

knowledge and love, and if we are to enter more fully into the mystery of His life and so hear Him more clearly, we must not try to walk this path alone. We need the spiritual support and companionship of others who are walking the same road. We need to share with them in conversation and study, and we need to pray with them, so that we ourselves can be comforted and healed of the hurt of our lives, and so that we can learn more about how to pray healing prayer.

We need community. Community may be just one other person, or two others or more. It need not be grandiose or complicated, and it probably is better if it is not. But to grow in this ministry we need others to pray with us regularly as well as the opportunity to pray with them. When I began to pray for people, I was blessed with a group of seven others who were similarly ministering inner healing prayer to suffering people; we met regularly every week for three hours at a time for a period of eighteen months to two years to pray with each other. I learned more in that group than I will ever be able to express to anyone—about the different ways a problem could be approached, about the different forms love can take, about the different kinds of problems people can have, but, most important, about the different ways in which I needed to be loved. During those meetings as we who ministered to others shared our problems with each other, I learned much wisdom and I was deeply healed. Now I find this same kind of experience through a national organization called the Association of Christian Therapists,[1] comprised of members of the helping professions as well as lay people, all of whom believe in healing prayer.

God is community—Father, Son, and Spirit, Three in One and One in Three—and somehow it is in community that He does His most wonderful works. As people dedicate themselves to each other, commit their lives in love to each other, and let their hearts be broken for each other, God heals. As I watch not only myself but others in these groups be healed in many different ways, a deep and unshakable faith based on real experience grows within me. It is on the basis of that faith that I minister to others today. And it is on the basis of that kind of experiential faith that any of us will become healed and healing members of the Kingdom of God.

Note

1. For more information on the Association of Christian Therapists, write to this address: 3700 East Avenue, Rochester, NY 14618; telephone: (716) 381-8590